HOW TO LIVE FOR FREE

HOW TO LIVE FOR FREE

80 WAYS TO SLASH YOUR SPENDING

STEPHEN GILES

Viva Books
New Delhi | Mumbai | Chennai | Kolkata
Bangalore | Hyderabad | Kochi | Guwahati

First Indian Edition 2010

VIVA BOOKS PRIVATE LIMITED

- 4737/23 Ansari Road, Daryaganj, New Delhi 110 002
  E-mail: vivadelhi@vivagroupindia.net, Tel. 42242200
- 76, Service Industries, Shirvane, Sector 1, Nerul, Navi Mumbai 400 706
  E-mail: vivamumbai@vivagroupindia.net, Tel. 27721273, 27721274
- Jamals Fazal Chambers, 26 Greams Road, Chennai 600 006
  E-mail: vivachennai@vivagroupindia.net, Tel. 28290304, 28294241
- B-103, Jindal Towers, 21/1A/3 Darga Road, Kolkata 700 017
  E-mail: vivakolkata@vivagroupindia.net, Tel. 22836381, 22816713
- 7, Sovereign Park Apartments, 56-58, K. R. Road, Basavanagudi, Bangalore 560 004
  E-mail: vivabangalore@vivagroupindia.net, Tel. 26607409, 26607410
- 101-102 Mughal Marc Apartments, 3-4-637 to 641, Narayanguda, Hyderabad 500 029
  E-mail: vivahyderabad@vivagroupindia.net, Tel. 27564481, 27564482
- Beevi Towers, First Floor, SRM Road, Kaloor, Kochi 682 018, Kerala
  E-mail: vivakochi@vivagroupindia.net, Tel: 0484-2403055, 2403056
- 232, GNB Road, Beside UCO Bank, Silpukhuri, Guwahati 781 003
  E-mail: vivaguwahati@vivagroupindia.net, Tel: 0361-2666386

www.vivagroupindia.com

Published by arrangement with

Crimson Publishing,
a division of Crimson Business Ltd
Westminster House, Kew Road
Richmond, Surrey TW9 2ND

ISBN : 978-81-309-1486-2

Published by Vinod Vasishtha for Viva Books Private Limited, 4737/23, Ansari Road, Daryaganj, New Delhi - 110 002.

Printed and bound by Raj Press, R-3, Inderpuri, New Delhi - 110 012.

FOR
ADA GILES

CONTENTS

ACKNOWLEDGEMENTS

This book would not have been possible without the assistance of the following people, all of whom I acknowledge with grateful thanks: Nikki Locke, Lucy Stone at CAT, Patrick Whetman at Goat Industries, Angi Davies at Liftshare, Stephen Gregory, Esme Barber, Roni Jay and especially Steve Fountain. Thanks also to the many people who came forward with tips, hints and suggestions.

INTRODUCTION

Q: DO YOU WANT TO LIVE FOR FREE?

A: THEN YOU NEED TO BUY THIS BOOK.

No, seriously. It might seem a bit cheeky to suggest that you should start off on a course of extreme frugality by investing in a book, but I can assure you this is money well spent – money that you will quickly recoup in significant and sustained savings.

Let's make it clear from the start, living for free is one heck of a hard slog. But it is just about possible – and if you don't believe me skip straight on to section six for an example of the kind of life you might expect. For most of us, however, this book isn't just about living without cash, it's about making the most of the cash that we have so that we can live free of unnecessary restrictions and of the chains of overwhelming financial commitment.

Because we work so hard for the money that we have, it's more important than ever to be sure that our hard-earned wages are maximised. This means analysing every area of household and personal expenditure and asking some serious questions about what you're paying for and where you should be making savings. But it also means becoming an expert in the long-neglected and misunderstood arts of blagging, ligging, scrounging and scavenging. It means never paying good money for something that can be won, begged for, borrowed or made.

The tangible benefits are all here, on every page there's a saving to be made – slashing hundreds, perhaps even thousands from your expenses each year. If, as a result of this book, you can cut even 20 per cent from your own living expenses, you can put that money towards something important like a holiday or car – you could even work 20 per cent less and spend that extra time with your family or friends instead.

All of the money-saving ideas within *How to Live For Free* are, of course, legal. They have been comprehensively researched – many are tried and tested favourites – and every section is accompanied by detailed notes on how to achieve the aim, the relative advantages and disadvantages, the initial and ongoing outlay (if any) and an indication of how much, on average, this idea may trim from your costs in five key areas: socialising; food and drink; household bills; clothes, toys & other items and sport & leisure.

The ideas range from eco-friendliness to fiscal wisdom and self-sufficiency via downright cheekiness, but each one aims to guide you towards a serious and achievable goal of freedom living. Each idea is given its own 'Freedom living score' that rates how far it will progress you towards the ultimate goal of living for free.

This book doesn't have purely 'green' credentials, nor does it pretend to offer a specific world outlook or a financial quick-fix. It is a compendium of suggestions for further research and investigation from across all of these areas and more. It will give you a starting point for your own journey into freedom living.

"That's all very well," I hear you cry, "but I can't spare the time for all these fancy ideas." And while it's true that some of the suggestions in this book will involve a bit of time, effort and commitment, most of them will fit extremely comfortably into the routine of normal life. The ideas in this book don't require any specialist skills or expertise, just a basic level of practicality, common sense and a desire to see every penny that you spend justifying its outlay.

There may be areas where you don't need to make changes, there may be areas where you are unwilling or unable to do so – perhaps because of a lack of space or resource – but I can guarantee that you'll find something in these pages which will save you money and take you a giant leap closer to living for free.

SECTION ONE

SOCIALISING

1 START A BARTERING COLLECTIVE – TRADE SERVICES AND SKILLS

Do you dream of a world without money – a society in which we are all free from the constraints of earning a crust and free to trade our services in an open and creative environment? Well, someone's already beaten you to it. LETS (Local Employment and Trading Systems, sometimes known as Local Enterprise and Trading Systems, Local Exchange and Trading Systems, or Local Economic Trading Systems) started life in a small community in Canada in the early 1980s as a way for local people to trade goods and services outside of the straitjacket of the national economy.

There are now around 2,000 LETS schemes across the world. In the UK alone more than 30,000 people are involved in about 300 schemes.

Each LETS scheme has its own rules, but in general the system works by creating a bespoke unit of currency and then issuing cheque books to its members with which they can 'buy' services from other members for an agreed 'fee'. No money changes hands between the participants, but everyone pays a nominal membership fee in hard currency to fund the administration of the scheme. Schemes are generally managed on a day-to-day basis by volunteers.

Nikki Locke was a key member of a LETS scheme established in Oswestry. Though the scheme has now closed, it once reached a peak of 100 active members and formed the basis of a crucial alternative local economy. So why did it close? "At its peak, when there was high unemployment, it worked well – it brought together a community of like-minded people," Nikki explains. "Now most people with practical skills are too busy earning money to get involved."

This highlights the greatest disadvantage of LETS, as those people with the time to spend on the scheme aren't necessarily the most skilled workers. Traders that tend to be successful as part of LETS – like builders, plumbers and electricians – find no shortage of paid work when the economy is booming. But even in the good times, there's scope for a LETS scheme to thrive, as long as it can find members who are willing to offer in-demand services like bookkeeping, gardening or painting and decorating.

It's not just a shortage of skills that threaten LETS schemes, there's also an assumption that schemes will take too much time to manage, which, as Nikki Locke explains, isn't really the case: "There is a shortage of people with the spare time and skills to commit to running a scheme, but our LETS scheme took a total of about 140 person hours a year to run. There were usually about five or six people in the main group, plus help from ordinary members, so it was probably less than two hours per person per month."

So if you've got a like-minded group of skilled individuals and you can summon sufficient enthusiasm to devote a couple of hours a month to running the group, what do you do next? The National Association of LETS schemes offers further information on starting your own LETS collective as well as more specific guidance on the legalities of trading schemes. Visit www.letslinkuk.net for more information.

The one essential attribute of a LETS scheme is a strong communitarian ethos – while it's vital that your group is structured correctly, it is more important that you make every member of the group feel like a key part. Creating a co-operative gives all members a role to play, and allows the community to build beyond simple trading into a self-supporting network.

ADVANTAGES: It's great for anyone with a rare (and consequently valuable) skill or trade. It's even better if you can extend your scheme to give members free access to a range of costly 'infrequent use' items like ladders, mowers etc.

DISADVANTAGES: Not a cost-effective option for those of us whose only saleable commodity is the ability to stand up straight. Also not an immediate guarantee of quality service, with much potential for awkwardness in the case of disputes.

INITIAL/ONGOING OUTLAY: cost of membership is approximately £10-£15 per year

POTENTIAL SAVING: A comprehensive scheme gives its members access to a huge range of skills, and the savings can run to thousands of pounds a year. Savings must, of course, be offset by the loss of income on any services you perform for other members of the scheme.

FREEDOM LIVING SCORE: 8 out of 10.

2 GO TO THE LIBRARY FOR BOOKS, INTERNET AND COURSES

Pity the poor library; under-funded, under-used and undervalued. They are widely viewed as draughty, forbidding places in which tramps seek refuge, old ladies do battle over the latest large-print Georgette Heyer and school kids pass notes while pretending to do their homework.

In reality, the vast majority of public libraries are modern, well-equipped and extremely useful resources for anyone wishing to live for free. It's not just the number of books available without charge, it's also the wide range of additional services, including internet access, reading groups, free story-time circles and activities for kids and readings from local poets and authors.

For a small fee there's a selection of videos, DVDs and CDs to hire, as well as language courses. Some libraries offer free courses, such as Welsh language courses in Welsh libraries, while others are the local centre for Learn Direct free literacy and numeracy courses (see adult education in section five).

In recent years, the free internet access in libraries, introduced through the People's Network scheme, has been a lifesaver for the crumbling system. Because these facilities are so popular, they are often over-subscribed and it can be hard to get access for more than an hour at a time, which means you have to be pretty focused in your browsing. Remember to take a pen drive with you to download anything you want to take away. And never use a public computer to send sensitive private data such as banking information.

In addition to the cost of hiring CDs and DVDs, there is usually a charge to borrow a book from outside your local council's area. This charge can vary from 80p right the way to a whopping £4 depending on where you live, though if you're astute enough to reside in Wales, inter-library loans are free.

Another way to side-step charges is through a students' scheme called SCONUL Access, which permits the members of nearly 200 participating academic libraries to borrow books from within the network for free. You need to be in education to access the facility, but this scheme opens up a huge network of resources.

ADVANTAGES: Access to a vast catalogue of books – including the latest hardback titles. There are often excellent reference and research facilities. Many larger libraries also stock an impressive selection of newspapers and periodicals. You can also get free literacy stuff and books to keep from the library for kids through the government's Bookstart scheme.

DISADVANTAGES: Some smaller libraries have short opening hours. Internet access is very popular and places are often limited. You may find yourself sitting next to someone giving off a strange smell and talking about the voices in their head. This person may be a librarian.

INITIAL OUTLAY: none

ONGOING OUTLAY: none (CDs/ DVDs and some inter-library loans etc. incur costs)

POTENTIAL SAVING: If you can train yourself to be inquisitive rather than acquisitive, then you'll save a small fortune at the library. The average hardback book costs in the region of £12-£15 and a chart CD will set you back £10. Take a look at the number of books you've bought and never read and the CDs you played just once. I guarantee that'll get you reaching for your library card.

FREEDOM LIVING SCORE: 10 out of 10

3 GET FREE CINEMA, THEATRE AND CONCERT TICKETS BY SETTING UP YOUR OWN LOCAL ARTS WEBSITE OR REVIEWING FOR A LOCAL NEWSPAPER

To get free access to arts events, you need to persuade the promoters that your views are respected. The most convincing way to do this is still to get into print courtesy of your local newspaper, but in the digital age, many local websites have been established for the purpose of providing views and information to locals and visitors, and if you can attract publicity to your website, you can present a pretty compelling case for your inclusion on press lists for all the local arts venues.

If you're interested in the theatre and your local venue deals mainly in touring productions, it might be worth contacting the touring company's press office direct, rather than dealing with the theatre.

In all cases, it's worth your while to show willing. Offer a press officer some advanced publicity (a preview) of their event on your website. This drums up interest in the event and boosts your chances of getting review tickets. Dealing with press offices is a matter of relationship building – if you help them shift a few more tickets for a slow-selling event they'll reward you with plum seats for the best shows/concerts.

As regards the nuts and bolts of establishing a site, you can actually set up a basic website for free using shareware downloaded from the internet. Most web hosting companies offer basic website templates for free to anyone who buys a domain name. If you've got a bit of design flair and basic computer skills, you can buy a do-it-yourself website in a box for around £25 from most computer stores which should suit your needs perfectly.

As for approaching newspapers, well that's a matter of trial and error – it's worth reading the paper's reviews, then writing something on spec that's in a similar format. Don't expect to get paid for the review, only a few papers have any kind of freelance budget any more, but you should at least get two tickets and have the cost of travel reimbursed. It's worth trying regional papers as well, as they may not have anyone covering your immediate area.

The final question is 'what do you write?' It's hard to find something new to say every time an amateur production of *Hobson's Choice* hits the stage, and reviewing theatre can be a hazardous profession unless you're always prepared to back up your comments. To steer clear of libel, remember the old journalists' maxim – 'you should only criticise the performance and never the performer'.

With film, it can be hard to get access for reviewing purposes, especially if you've only managed to make it onto the cinema's 'free list' – the collective of spongers and freeloaders, including staff, that can go to films for nothing on production of a pass. Many new releases at the cinema are specified on the listings as 'free list suspended', which means everyone has to pay to get in. Spoilsports.

ADVANTAGES: Setting up your own site is good for your status and makes you feel important. Getting into print can open doors – if you've got a portfolio of work that can help you get other work, whether reviewing for other papers or possibly features work on the paper you're reviewing for.

DISADVANTAGES: If you're commissioned to do a review you don't get to choose what you'll be watching. Brace yourself for some truly awful (free) nights out.

INITIAL OUTLAY: £25 approx (setting up website), cost of calls/letters to newspapers and cinemas/ theatres

ONGOING OUTLAY: minimal admin costs

POTENTIAL SAVING: Depending on how often you go to arts events, the savings could be anything up to £300 per year at least.

FREEDOM LIVING SCORE: 7 out of 10

4 GIVE AND RECEIVE FOR FREE ON WEBSITES LIKE FREECYCLE.ORG

Established in May 2003, Freecycle is now a global phenomenon, but it has managed to maintain a slightly subversive, underground ethos by focusing its attention on local self-policing groups of individuals who offer goods freely (and for free) amongst themselves. Membership is free and open to all.

So if, for example, you're looking to offload anything from computer equipment to electrical appliances and furniture, get involved in your local community through the freecycle network. You'll find a wealth of like-minded individuals online, all of whom will have something worth passing on to someone. And if there is no local community, consider starting one and invite your friends and colleagues to join.

The main rules of participation are that no money passes hands, no illegal items can be offered and the receiver always collects. Beyond that, it's not a 'trading' service in the same manner as LETS, as it's possible to receive without ever giving, but to fully participate in the communitarian ethos of freecycle, it's worth throwing yourself heart and soul into the process. You never know what you'll find.

ADVANTAGES: In essence, freecycle and its imitators are helping to create a world in which nothing need ever be thrown away. And it certainly bears out the adage that one man's tat is another man's table lamp.

DISADVANTAGES: As an internet-based phenomenon, freecycle is beset by two of the web's greatest ills, spam and sharks. The spam is an inevitable part of being included in a community, and depending on the size of your local group, you may feel overwhelmed by the number of offers and wants you receive on a daily basis. There are also some unscrupulous users who are trying to sniff out valuable items to sell on – there's not much you can do about these blighters, except stick together as a community and try to root them out.

INITIAL/ONGOING OUTLAY: none

POTENTIAL SAVING: limitless, if you strike it lucky, but that's not really the point.

FREEDOM LIVING SCORE: 10 out of 10

5 TRICKS TO AVOID EVER PAYING FOR A ROUND OF DRINKS

It's important to be sociable, even if you're living on a zero budget, but trips to the pub are fraught with potentially crippling drinks bills. These can be avoided but only through the judicious use of monitoring and surveillance tactics. While it's important to avoid meeting the cost of everyone else's drinks, you must also avoid looking like too much of a skinflint, otherwise you'll just stop being invited along.

The following tips should help to ensure you rarely pay for a round, but ought to keep you in the good books of friends and family:

A Pub first, bar last. Make sure you're the first one of your party to reach the pub door as this shows willing. Then hold the door open for everyone else to pass through – this shows a generosity of spirit but it will also ensure you are always the last person to reach the bar. By this time ordering will be underway and your selfless gesture will earn you your first drink.

B Drink with a large, affluent crowd. The people to avoid socially are those who divide bills down to three decimal points. You need to ingratiate yourself with a sizeable party of people who think nothing of throwing in an extra drink for the pretty barmaid. Large crowds are generally good, as the drinks rota is complex and your lack of contribution will, in the short term at least, go unnoticed.

C Drink aware. It stands to reason that you'll spend less if you drink less, but it's equally important to drink at a different pace from the crowd. If you dovetail your drinking to fit with the majority, you will inevitably end up trapped with a large round. If you can tailor your drinking to a smaller subsection within the crowd, you're more likely to be able to manage your place in the round-buying rota, while still enjoying the anonymity of being part of the larger crowd.

D Get out while the going's good. If all else fails and the bell hasn't tolled before your round is due, tactical withdrawal may be your only option. This, again, is a matter of timing. Your excuse must be plausible and sudden – a forgotten promise to be elsewhere, realisation of an early start in the morning, even a hastily arranged phone call. You must offer to buy your round before you leave, but to ensure this offer isn't taken up, you'll need to make it while everyone's glasses are relatively full. Being thus deprived of the chance to be generous towards your friends, you can leave with a clear conscience and the assurance that you will buy the first round next time. Unless you happen to be holding the door that is . . .

ADVANTAGES: You drink cheap

DISADVANTAGES: You look cheap

INITIAL/ONGOING OUTLAY: zero, in an ideal world.

POTENTIAL SAVINGS: Even working on the assumption that you will have to buy the odd drink, these tips should at least halve the cost of a night out.

FREEDOM LIVING SCORE: 5 out of 10

6 SELL ITEMS THROUGH FREE ADS

The eBay generation may have cornered the online marketplace, but it's important to remember that there's a well-established trading network for low priced items in the various free ads publications that you'll find all over the country. While eBay and its clones are great for collectors, or people on the hunt for a new or nearly new bargain, it's not a cost effective place to sell your more tired possessions.

Most free-ad newspapers (easily identified by the garish hue of their paper) offer a free section for people posting low value goods, and local/regional newspapers often have similar free advertising sections. If you insist that the buyer collects the item, you can clear a wide range of items and make a veritable fortune from stuff that would otherwise be cluttering your crawl-space. If you can break up a collection of items without decreasing the value – like an old dinner service for example – then it's worth your while avoiding the advertising costs.

ADVANTAGES: If the altruism of freecycle isn't for you, or if you want to make a few quid from something that's worthless to you, free ads are a lifesaver.

DISADVANTAGES: Low value items are hard to shift at the best of times, and the kind of people who want to pay good money for your broken toaster may not be the kind of people you want in your house.

INITIAL/ONGOING OUTLAY: none

POTENTIAL SAVING: a paid-for ad in a newspaper or shop window can cost anything from £1 per week to £5 per week.

FREEDOM LIVING SCORE: 8 out of 10

7 CREATE A ROTA-SYSTEM BABYSITTING CIRCLE

It can be a nightmare to find a good babysitter, especially as the traditional route of employing a responsible, reliable teenager seems to be fraught with hazard and chronically short of credible candidates.

In the spirit of the LETS scheme, an increasing number of people form their own babysitting circles of anything up to a dozen members. This system allows you to earn credits when babysitting for others, which can then be 'spent' when you fancy a night out without the kids yourself. As with LETS, no actual money changes hands – all new members start with a certain number of credits.

Another similarity with LETS is that the structure and rules of the scheme are vital. It goes without saying that all participants should be known to each other and trustworthy, but it's worth laying down some rules of etiquette at the outset. For example, a six-hour babysitting session with an insomniac toddler is unlikely to have a value equivalent to a two-hour daytime session minding a nine year old. So some kind of points tally must be set and all members must keep full records of the times, durations and nature of the babysitting undertaken.

The scheme should be fairly easy to administer as long as all participants play a fairly active role earning and spending babysitting credits. To make the process even simpler, a pair of far-sighted parents have set up a babysitting circle administration website [www.mynightoff.com] which allows groups to create a bespoke template which all members can then access to book slots.

ADVANTAGES: A babysitting circle established among a group of friends who know each other well should work brilliantly, saving lots of money and stress.

DISADVANTAGES: The reality is that even among friends we have widely differing ideas of what constitutes good parenting. This can lead to possible conflict if you choose to avoid babysitting for a particular member of the group or having them look after your brood.

INITIAL OUTLAY: minimal administration costs

ONGOING OUTLAY: none

POTENTIAL SAVING: One to two nights a month at approximately £5 per hour equals an annual saving of around £400-£500.

FREEDOM LIVING SCORE: 8 out of 10

8 CREATE AN AFTER-SCHOOL CLUB

In the same way that a babysitting circle has the capacity to thrive when established by a group of trusted friends, an after-school club, or breakfast club, can function very well when established in a tight-knit community. To work effectively, it depends on the availability of a responsible supervising parent each day and unless everyone lives in mansions the group size needs to be manageable – no more than five or six children.

While it's essential for parents to establish ground rules for the structure, management and operation of the after-school club, the actual nature of the club should be pretty fluid – there's a whole range of alternatives from cooking clubs to reading groups to gardening clubs – anything in fact that reinforces your children's learning and encourages an interest. The larger the group and the more specialised the activity, the greater the likelihood of complications, so if you're aiming to set up a group on a small scale it's best to aim low in terms of the range of facilities offered.

Larger and more ambitious groups do work, but these are best planned in conjunction with a school, and ideally they will take place on school property under correct supervision and within the terms of the school's insurance.

ADVANTAGES: If you're lucky enough to have a self-supporting group of friends then an after-school club is a natural progression from the babysitting circle. If the club is properly managed, no one should feel put upon and your children will thrive in a safe environment.

DISADVANTAGES: In our increasingly litigious world, most people would be concerned about taking responsibility for another child's welfare or handing their welfare to someone without proper training or criminal checks. It goes without saying (hopefully) that you should never arrange to leave your children in the care of someone you don't trust implicitly.

INITIAL/ONGOING OUTLAY: additional cost of drinks/ food for children (estimate a fee of approx £3 each child per session)

POTENTIAL SAVING: £10 per child per week approx.

FREEDOM LIVING SCORE: 7 out of 10

9 DO A CAR SHARE FOR LONG JOURNEYS

Car sharing is simply when two or more people share a journey, whether this is travelling on holiday, to university, to a festival or to the airport. According to statistics produced by car sharing website liftshare.org, at present there are 38 million empty seats on UK roads every day. In 2005, more than 60 per cent of the cars on our roads had only one occupant and 85 per cent of commuters travelled alone by car. A two per cent rise in occupancy would result in a reduction of five billion kilometres of road travel.

Car sharing isn't just about long-haul travel – you can car share for any journey you make. It allows people to benefit from the obvious convenience of the car, while reducing the costs and alleviating the associated problems of congestion and pollution. It's also a great way to save money and reduce your carbon footprint.

The website *lift*share.org was originally established in 1998 by student Ali Clabburn. Now, the largest car sharing network in the UK, *lift*share's mission is to "encourage and enable more efficient use of the car". *Lift*share's online network introduces people travelling in the same direction at the same time so they can travel together for their daily commute or for leisure.

According to *lift*share, a typical car-sharer will save themselves around £1,000 and 1 tonne of CO2 per year by sharing their daily journey - about 10 per cent of an individual's carbon footprint. One *lift*share member saved more than £15,000 in travel costs over five years.

ADVANTAGES: There are many, including saving money and saving the planet, as well as cutting down on all car expenses and turning travelling into a social networking exercise.

DISADVANTAGES: Like all social networking, there's a risk involved. While liftshare wisely detaches itself from any responsibility for who you choose to share your car with, you will need to be careful about selecting a travelling companion. Be sensible about it – never give out too much personal information in advance, meet in a public place and if you have the slightest reservations about your car-sharing buddy, make other arrangements immediately. But don't be put off: as a general rule, the worst that can happen is that you'll be stuck in a conversation about Viking re-enactments for four hours.

INITIAL/ONGOING OUTLAY: none for the free web matching service

POTENTIAL SAVING: the more people you can get to share your car the cheaper/ safer it is. A journey with three passengers will cut your costs by 75 per cent, getting you from one end of the country to the other for £10.

FREEDOM LIVING SCORE: 8 out of 10.

10 CAR SHARE FOR WORK OR SCHOOL RUNS

As mentioned above, car sharing isn't just about one-off journeys, it's also feasible to organise car shares for regular journeys, including the daily commute and the school run.

In addition to its free public access network, *lift*share has developed a consultancy service for business, providing schemes to more than 900 clients, helping them to increase their level of social responsibility and demonstrate a commitment to the environment by cutting congestion and pollution. With additional incentives such as 'guaranteed ride home' schemes and reserved 'green' parking spaces in priority locations, employees of those companies with schemes are reaping the benefits.

In the city, where parking is at a premium, the reduction of a car parking facility by just 50 spaces could save a business up to £2,000 per space. By introducing a car sharing scheme, employers can save money on car park maintenance costs, capital expenditure, administration costs, security, lighting, CCTV and control of unauthorised parking.

It also helps employers to raise their corporate profile by demonstrating their level of social responsibility and their commitment to the environment, cut congestion and pollution. Such schemes can even help to improve the general well being of staff by building a social network and creating stronger ties between colleagues.

*Lift*share Solutions provides public and private schemes to a range of clients from multi-national businesses and local authorities through to small community groups. Even if you don't have the budget to engage *lift*share Solutions, you can formalise your own relaxed car-sharing scheme centred on a school, workplace, football supporters' club or other group.

ADVANTAGES: For employers and schools, the benefits include cutting congestion and potentially reducing the need for parking facilities. It's a good exercise in social responsibility and community cohesion for all involved. Some local authorities, such as South Gloucestershire, have introduced priority lanes on dual carriageways for cars with more than one occupant travelling during peak commuter hours.

DISADVANTAGES: There aren't many, though car sharing does seem to work best when everyone involved works regular hours (for example council staff) as there's less time wasted hanging around while your colleagues finish their day's work.

INITIAL/ONGOING OUTLAY: dependent on circumstances

POTENTIAL SAVING: again, this depends on the number of participants per car and the length of the journey, but savings can range from £20-40 per week.

FREEDOM LIVING SCORE: 6 out of 10

11 DON'T HAVE DINNER PARTIES HAVE POT LUCK DINNERS

Just because you're cutting back on your spending, you don't need to rein in your socialising. If you host a dinner party for all your friends the bill can run into hundreds of pounds, unless you've followed all the instructions in section two (see below) and can provide the vegetables, meat and alcohol from your own reserves. Even so, a dozen hungry guests use up a lot of valuable resources.

That's why a pot luck dinner makes so much more sense than a traditional dinner party. Basically, a pot luck is a dinner in which each guest brings one dish – a starter, a main course or a pudding. The greatest skill involved in planning a pot luck dinner is project management. You must ensure that the meal isn't a conceptual nightmare, with one pizza and eleven desserts (though that's my idea of a perfect menu). So that means subdividing the requirements on a person-by-person basis. The best way to do this is to base it on people's cooking ability. Most people can buy or cook a starter or dessert easily and without fuss, but a decent main course takes time and skill.

With a guest list of 12 friends, you will have four or five good cooks, each of whom should bring a constituent part of the main course, which in the case of a traditional roast meal means a further subdivision between meat, vegetables and potatoes. It's often better to go for cuisine that traditionally involves many dishes, like Indian, Chinese, Greek or North African food. Everyone else can be split between starters and desserts. If there's someone who genuinely can't or won't cook, you can set them the task of bringing cheese and biscuits or even providing extra cutlery, tablecloths, rolls or alcohol.

As a rule, and in the general spirit of community, everyone should bring a bottle too. If you don't have the cutlery or crockery to cope with such a large party, get everyone to weigh in with their own bits and pieces, or buy extra from a charity shop – the great bonus of a pot luck is that as everyone is so relaxed by the spirit of co-operation, no one bothers about such insignificant details.

Assuming your pot luck is a success, you'll have to make your own contributions to other dinners in turn, of course, but the cost will be spread over the year, allowing you to juggle your home-grown resources to maximum effect and minimal impact on your low-cost larder.

ADVANTAGES: Pot luck dinners create a great feeling of community, no one feels put-upon and the host, for once, isn't left with a load of dirty dishes, as these can be taken home at the end.

DISADVANTAGES: Some people feel that the only true spirit of pot luck is to let people get whatever they want without instruction, believing that the organic results are much more interesting. Anyone who has ever eaten a dozen different types of quiche in one evening would disagree.

INITIAL OUTLAY: ideally zero for the host, no more than £5 per guest

ONGOING OUTLAY: £5 per party

POTENTIAL SAVING: In terms of time and effort, £50-£100 per dinner party.

FREEDOM LIVING SCORE: 7 out of 10

12 SET UP A PROGRESSIVE DINNER PARTY CIRCLE

A variation on the 'pot luck' theme, the progressive dinner party, otherwise known in the States as a 'Condo Conga' or notably in Tim Firth's play of the same name as a 'Safari Party', involves the same principle of co-operative cooking, but with the added bonus of co-operative hosting as well.

Progressive parties work well among groups of friends who live close together, but who don't necessarily all have big houses or the space to host a large party. Those people with smaller houses begin the party with appetisers and aperitifs, then the group switches location to a larger residence for starter, then switches again for main course, and so on until another smaller venue can step in for coffee and liqueurs at the end of the evening.

Logistically, few people are likely to stand more than four or five changes of venue, even if the houses are all in the same street, but as with pot luck dinners, it cuts down on the daunting scale of a dinner party and minimises the costs as well.

ADVANTAGES: You can walk off each course. If you aren't comfortable in someone's home – whether because of the doggy smells, the decor or the dust – you haven't got to stay all night.

DISADVANTAGES: It'll be hard to convince any non-participants that a progressive party isn't a euphemism for wife-swapping. Also, five houses have to be frantically tidied for guests rather than just one.

INITIAL OUTLAY: the host pays for their course only, at about £5 per guest

ONGOING OUTLAY: none

POTENTIAL SAVING: about £50 per dinner party.

FREEDOM LIVING SCORE: 6 out of 10 (plus a point for the exercise)

SECTION TWO

FOOD & DRINK

13 GROW ALL THE VEGETABLES YOU'LL NEED WITHOUT A GARDEN

When we think about providing our own food, it's easy to conjure up the image of 1970s sitcom *The Good Life* – a great big cultivated garden brimming with produce and a huge allotment thrown in. But the reality for most of us is a significantly reduced circumstance. Should it naturally follow that we have reduced ambitions? Not a bit of it.

Even if you've got the tiniest of postage stamp sized yards, you can make the most of your space to produce a plethora of produce. The trick is to think laterally (not to mention vertically and horizontally). Maximising space is the key, and good use of the area should go hand in hand with selection of the best plants, fruit and vegetables for your garden. If you've got no garden at all it's even theoretically possible to grow some fruit and vegetables indoors – a window box of herbs and lettuce should be within everyone's grasp.

If you're planting straight into the ground, you'll need to bear in mind soil type as well as the important factor of the garden's aspect – which areas are in sun and shade, which are protected from the elements and which are exposed. Container gardening, in which the produce is grown in anything from a tub to a Wellington boot, depends less on aspect as most containers can be shifted around according to the conditions.

A small yard of approximately five metres by three metres should give enough opportunity to grow a family's produce, providing it is well planned. Beans, peas, soft fruit trees, apple and pear trees can be trained against a fence to minimise the space used. Potatoes can be grown in a barrel or a raised bed, herbs and tomatoes are attractive components of hanging baskets and cabbages, lettuces and carrots will grow happily in clumps within pots and tubs.

When choosing tubs and pots, go for something that allows for drainage – strong wooden troughs or oak tubs are good, as are porous terracotta pots. You can make a whole range of wooden planters and troughs for very little money and they look pretty handsome when they're filled with trailing produce. But remember that anything can be used as long as it drains well, from milk churns to wheelbarrows, from baby baths to stock pots.

ADVANTAGES: Container gardening allows you to micro-manage your produce. You can bring stuff indoors during extreme cold and heat and you can use vegetables and herbs to decorate your garden.

DISADVANTAGES: If your main concern is yields, container gardening isn't the best option – go for an allotment instead and stick to neat rows.

INITIAL OUTLAY: seeds/compost/containers will cost approximately £15

ONGOING OUTLAY: none

POTENTIAL SAVING: £250-£300 per year approx

FREEDOM LIVING SCORE: 8 out of 10

14 TURN YOUR GARDEN INTO A SPECIALIST VEGETABLE PATCH

If you've got a patch of soil that you're planning to turn over to vegetable or fruit growing, or if you can get hold of an allotment, you've got to think about how to get the best of the space available.

If you plant row upon row of potatoes, you will undoubtedly get a lot of practical produce (providing you like potatoes of course), but spuds are ten a penny, or at least ten a pound, and can be bought or bartered anywhere. If you're on an allotment, there's likely to be a frantic trade in vegetables, as crop yields are invariably higher than one household's needs. So you need to think carefully about how you're going to trade, and whether you can produce a commodity that's so rare, it can be traded for all the common or garden vegetables you need.

While everyone else is sweating over their carrots and runner beans, focus your attentions on asparagus, spinach, globe and Jerusalem artichokes, garlic and rocket. Specialising in 'deli-veg' gives you the edge over your fellow horticulturalists, cuts the cost of buying these pricey but delicious vegetables and means you'll always be in demand when it comes to swapping time.

Think also about how you can raise the profile of the humble vegetable after it's grown – garlic can be smoked (in a smokery, not a pipe) for a really intense flavour, while a Jerusalem artichoke makes a cracking potato substitute, both for chips and, along with beetroot, as thick-cut, hand-fried crisps.

ADVANTAGES: You'll corner the market in fancy foods and mark yourself out as a true specialist.

DISADVANTAGES: Perennials like artichokes and asparagus take a couple of years to bed in, so they are a long term bet. Specialist vegetables sometimes require very specific soil conditions, so plan carefully. And finally, if your fellow allotment holders are all wizened old men in their late 80s, be warned that they might tell you to stick your rocket where the sun doesn't shine.

INITIAL OUTLAY: seeds, off-cuts etc. £10-£15

ONGOING OUTLAY: none

POTENTIAL SAVING: £250 per year

FREEDOM LIVING SCORE: 8 out of 10

15 BREW YOUR OWN ALCOHOL

If you really want to save money on alcohol, your best bet is to avoid drinking it altogether. Winemaking is a rewarding and sometimes challenging hobby that can produce spectacular results but which can also cost a lot of money to set up if you follow expert guidance to the letter and invest in fermentation jars, thermometers and other assorted items from Frankenstein's laboratory. While beer brewing is generally an easier task, it still requires a fair degree of preparation, and unless you can grow the ingredients yourself, it can be hard to source all the constituent parts.

If you are serious about making wine, your best bet is to broadcast this fact widely to friends and family and get them to buy all the necessary equipment over time as Christmas and birthday presents, otherwise you'll struggle to make the kit pay for itself. You can always repay kindly relatives in homemade wine when you've perfected the art.

If you're in a hurry, it is possible to cut corners, although the results may be less than spectacular. In this case it may be better to think more in terms of augmenting low-grade alcohol rather than trying to find it for free. For example, dirt-cheap spirits can be considerably enlivened by the addition of herbs and hedgerow fruits – sloe gin being a particularly good example. In my experience, sloes are also a fine basic ingredient of wine, as are another common foraged fruit, elderberries. In both cases, these freely abundant fruits can produce wonderfully deep, rich, port-like wine.

If, however, you're just looking for bargain basement plonk that tastes OK and achieves the desired effect, there follows a knock-out recipe for knock-out apple wine – recommended by a die-hard freedom living expert who claims to have saved a small fortune thanks to this simple recipe:

APPLE TIPPLE

30 litre food grade plastic bucket with lid
20 litres of apple juice (If you can't juice your own apples then supermarket value brands are the best bet)
2kg sugar
10 litres of water
2 teaspoons yeast
Suitable steriliser for the bucket (eg sodium meta bisulphate)

Method: Sterilise your bucket and rinse thoroughly. Add the sugar and a kettle of boiled water then agitate until the sugar has dissolved. Add the apple juice and then top up with water until you have 30 litres. Add the yeast then wait approximately six weeks or until the liquid is clear. You'll then have an apple wine/cider of approximately 11 per cent alcohol content. This is particularly tasty with a splash of sparkling spring water. It's a great everyday drink which can also be used as a present for friends – it's also ideal for trading on the allotment for tips, seeds and vegetables. Source apples for juicing from friends with apple trees – there are always more windfalls than they can cope with.

ADVANTAGES: If you can invest the time and money in equipment, you can produce excellent wines and beer with the minimum of ongoing outlay. Some fruit wines are absolutely delicious.

DISADVANTAGES: Expensive set-up costs and long storage time – most home-brewed wines should be left for at least three months before drinking. And sometimes the results can be absolutely shocking. If you're determined to do the whole thing yourself, be prepared also to spend a long time mashing, pulping, peeling and juicing fruit.

INITIAL OUTLAY: anything from £50-£250 depending on your ambition

ONGOING OUTLAY: minimal for sugar and yeast

POTENTIAL SAVING: depending on typical consumption, from £200-£500 per year.

FREEDOM LIVING SCORE: 6 out of 10

16 GO HEDGEROW HARVESTING FOR FRUIT TO MAKE PIES, CORDIALS AND JAMS

Hedgerow harvesting is a deeply satisfying pursuit for anyone dedicated to living for free. It isn't just the concept of picking nature's bounty without spending a penny of hard-earned cash that's so appealing, but also the image of countless jams, chutneys, cordials, soups and puddings that can be derived from berries, leaves, flowers and fungi.

We might associate hedgerow harvesting with the autumn months, but in truth there's something to be snaffled from springtime onwards if you know where to look. Start with elderflowers for cordial and 'champagne' – though don't take too many or there won't be anything left for elderberry cordial in the autumn. Nettles spring up with alarming regularity as soon as the sun begins to get warmer, and they're a great, nutritious ingredient for soups (see below). Wild strawberries and cherries are excellent summer fruits if you can get to them before the birds.

Mushrooms are, if you'll pardon the pun, in a field of their own and need to be treated with great care by the novice forager. Take a good field guide with you and make sure you're certain which type of mushroom you've picked before eating it. Save a little bit back just in case you get sick, it will help identification (of the mushroom, not of your body) later if needed.

The Food Standards Agency encourages hedgerow harvesting as a natural way to supplement our daily diet, but it also offers the following advice to foragers:

When identifying any berry, fruit or fungi, check several features to be certain (look at leaf, flower, colour, shape and season). If you're unsure, avoid it. Never collect plants and berries growing in industrial or polluted areas or near busy roads. If you do go foraging, only take what you need – always give the plant a fair chance to reproduce. Under the 1981 Wildlife and Countryside Act it is illegal to uproot any wild plant without the permission of the owner. You should never pick any rare or endangered wild plants under any circumstances.

If you stick to the above rules of good practice you'll have many happy hours foraging and harvesting – try canal towpaths, cycleways and byways for the best and cleanest produce. The following is a favourite tried-and-tested foraging recipe:

NETTLE SOUP

20-30 nettle plants
One leek or onion, finely chopped
One potato, diced
One diced carrot, swede or parsnip depending on preference

1 litre chicken stock (or vegetable stock if preferred)
Oil or butter

Method: Sweat the onion in the oil/butter, add par-boiled potatoes and root vegetables and simmer together for a few minutes. Carefully wash and pick the nettle leaves and then add these to the pot. Add the stock and allow everything to simmer for about 25 minutes. Finish off with salt and pepper or add some yoghurt/crème fraiche to suit and then blend to required consistency.

ADVANTAGES: Foraging is a satisfying, free and incredibly versatile method of boosting your larder all year round.

DISADVANTAGES: Fungi and berries are potentially hazardous if you don't take due care, but as long as you follow FSA recommendations you should be fine. The greatest disadvantage is that so many people now enjoy hedgerow harvesting you might struggle to find a free spot. If you do identify a plentiful source of berries, freeze some of your pickings immediately to ensure you always have a good, fresh stock available.

INITIAL/ONGOING OUTLAY: for picking and eating, zero. Minimal outlay for making jams and chutneys.

POTENTIAL SAVING: £50 per year

FREEDOM LIVING SCORE: 10 out of 10

17 NO MORE COFFEE CULTURE – DRINK SAMPLES IN STORE

One of the greatest cons of modern society is the growth of the coffee culture. The proliferation of coffee shops has created a civilisation dependent on costly choco-mocha-lattes with hazelnut dusting. While there's never been anything wrong with taking a pause for a quick brew while out shopping, this has now become a miniature meal in itself, with inflated prices to match. There's a difference between pausing for refreshment and burying your head in an oversized bowl of caffeinated froth and that difference could save you a fortune.

For starters you need to analyse the coffee buying experience – in general this consists of queuing for some considerable hours in a dark coffee shop to then spend five minutes sipping an already-cold coffee while clashing elbows with the fraught shopper next to you. All the good tables are taken by out of work actors pretending to write novels on their I-Books. It's not a value for money situation.

So your best bet is to focus on the 'refreshment' part of the phrase 'refreshment break'. If you need a caffeine hit, head to a delicatessen, or a retail coffee shop chain where the free samples of coffee are plentiful and the queues are short.

If, on the other hand, you just need a cool glass of water, go to the bank. Most banks have water coolers for customer use, and it's absolutely fine to have a couple of cups while you browse through the latest financial services products. Big department stores and Marks & Spencer are also good bets if you're just after a quick gulp of water.

Some places actively encourage the free consumption of beverages. Members of the free Ikea family card scheme [see www.ikea.com for stores and opening info] are entitled to free tea and coffee in the store's restaurants from Monday to Friday.

ADVANTAGES: You save money, time and the inconvenience of queuing in the 'relaxed' environment of a coffee shop.

DISADVANTAGES: Depending on how much coffee/water you tend to drink, you may have to spread yourself out around the various free sample emporiums in your locality – which won't help much if you live in a village.

INITIAL/ONGOING OUTLAY: none

POTENTIAL SAVING: A minimum of £100 per year

FREEDOM LIVING SCORE: 8 out of 10

18 SNACK FROM DELI COUNTERS AND AT PROMOTIONAL STANDS – ESPECIALLY GOOD AT CASH & CARRY STORES

Getting a hot lunch every day can add a good £15 per week to your outgoings as a minimum, as well as eating into your lunch break while you queue with the world and his wife for service. But if you're lucky enough to live or work in a big town, or within easy distance of a superstore, you can access free, hot food on a daily basis for no cost at all. Welcome to the world of the in-store demonstration.

The best source of demonstration food is the cash and carry store. You will need to organise (free) membership to get access to the in-store delights, but once you're there get set for a feeding frenzy as a whole range of hot snacks, from pizzas to pasta via meatballs and rollmop herrings are generally on offer. Unlike the bafflingly small portions in supermarkets, these are bulk samples. In the course of a trip around the store, it is possible to run through all three courses of a good-sized lunch.

If you're on a lighter diet, or you just fancy grazing as you browse, then supermarket deli counters, town-centre delicatessens and butchers' shops are all regular sources of on-the-counter freebies.

ADVANTAGES: You get to sample a range of food for free while giving the bored shop assistant something to do for five minutes.
Everyone's happy.

DISADVANTAGES: As with the free drinks above, it's possible to build up a potentially damaging reputation as a scavenger. Unlike drinks, snack foods are a better bet for a quick 'walk-by swoop' at the deli counter, allowing you to grab a handful of treats and make your get-away unnoticed. Also, living off snack treats may not constitute a balanced diet.

INITIAL/ONGOING OUTLAY: none

POTENTIAL SAVING: @ £15 per week for one year, £780

FREEDOM LIVING SCORE: 8 out of 10

19 GO FISH – HOW TO CATCH A VARIETY OF FISH AND SHELLFISH RELIABLY AND FREELY

Give a man a fish and he'll feed his family for a day, give him a rod and he'll spend the day fishing instead. But the law of averages dictates that he'll actually catch something at some stage. It's important to establish the difference between an angler and a fisherman at this point – rather like somebody who goes paint-balling differs from a soldier. Anglers fish for sport, while fishermen fish for fish. We need only concern ourselves with the latter here.

Rivers in most parts of the UK are controlled by the Environment Agency. You'll need a rod licence to fish these waters legally, as well as a permit from whoever owns the land you are fishing from, and there is a closed season on rivers from March to June each year. While it's not strictly illegal to keep the freshwater fish you catch, it can be frowned upon by sporting anglers. Check out the Environment Agency's web pages for anglers for full details of where to fish inland. Offshore sea fishing doesn't require a licence and you can keep whatever you catch, so if you've got a mate with a boat, that's the safest way to go.

The type of fishing method you use depends on the type of fish you are after – some keep close to the seabed, some swim free. The former are more likely to be caught in a static net or pot and the latter on a hooked line, but net fishing is also pretty profitable for catching fish like herring and mackerel that swim in large shoals.

Back on dry land, it's worth checking out the coastline at low tide for any shellfish and crustaceans that may be going begging. Mussels, clams, whelks, cockles and even crabs can be picked up easily this way and all make delicious and nutritious foodstuffs.

Never collect shellfish from somewhere built-up, or from an area close to a sewage outfall (for obvious reasons), don't eat any seafood that's dead before you cook it. If the pre-cooked shellfish gives some resistance when you try to open it, it's still alive; if it opens easily, it's already dead and should be discarded.

ADVANTAGES: As with any natural resource, fish and shellfish are a great bonus if you're living on a budget. And it's good for your brain.

DISADVANTAGES: Rules, regulations and anglers make fishing for food a bit of a chore in the UK, but sea fishing retains some of the glamour of the good old days.

INITIAL OUTLAY: fishing rod/nets approx. £25-£100

ONGOING OUTLAY: a licence for freshwater fishing costs up to £66.50 (2007/08 prices) per year. Anyone under 12 or over 65 can fish without a licence.

POTENTIAL SAVING: If you eat the government's recommended minimum of two portions of fish a week, you could save anything from £250-£500 per year by catching your own.

FREEDOM LIVING SCORE: 9 out of 10

20 SHOOT WILD ANIMALS

The rules on shooting animals for food are as complex as the rules on gun ownership. It's not possible to give full guidance on the ins and outs of the system here, so before you even think about either owning a gun or killing wildlife, consult an expert. Good places to start are www.defra.gov.uk for the government angle and www.basc.org.uk, the website of the British Association for Shooting and Conservation, which gives a broader industry perspective.

The basic ground rules for shooting wildlife are that most wild birds and mammals are protected in the UK, even on private land. Three categories of animals can be shot: wildfowl (including ducks, geese and woodcock) when they are not in a 'close' or breeding season; pests such as crows, pigeons and magpies may be shot by authorised persons under licence from the government; game species, such as pheasant, deer, hares, partridges and grouse may be shot, but again these have specific close seasons depending on species and breeding pattern.

Although this might be a point of argument in the bars of Islington, there is a close link between shooting and conservation, and many of the people who shoot in the UK have a vested interest in the conservation of the species. Farmers who send cattle to slaughter aren't acting irresponsibly, they're just managing the breed. The same can be said of legal, authorised shooting.

Of course, there are still people who take matters into their own hands, shooting pigeons or shooting and trapping rabbits/hares on common land for the pot. This is a dangerous pastime, not least because of the legal implications for anyone who breaks a walker's ankle with a trap, or takes someone's eye out with an airgun pellet. The best bet is to get decent advice, proper training and effective supervision – then get friendly with a farmer and you've got a ready source of game quarry to aim at.

ADVANTAGES: Sourcing our own food is a natural instinct. Shooting for sport is also a fine skill to master, albeit a difficult and fairly expensive one.

DISADVANTAGES: Shooting is an activity dogged by controversy and misconceptions. If you shoot to eat, you've also got to master the skills of skinning and butchering your kill.

INITIAL/ONGOING OUTLAY: You don't need a game licence in England or Wales, but you do in Scotland. Once you have the necessary gun licence, you can buy a shotgun for anything between £600 and £1,000 new.

POTENTIAL SAVING: If you shoot all your meat, you could save up to £1,000 a year.

FREEDOM LIVING SCORE: 7 out of 10

21 COLLECT AND COOK ROAD KILL

Foraging takes many forms, and while some people might think it is distasteful to eat something that's got tyre marks running along its back, there is a growing movement behind the argument that road kill is a perfectly legitimate and safe source of free meat.

Let's look at the legality first. Even though some of the animals accidentally killed on our roads are protected from hunters while alive, there is no law forbidding the consumption of their carcasses. In the USA, this is a grey area, as some drivers have been found using their vehicles as a hunting weapon, so some states have enforced a ban. But UK law currently allows all road kill to be consumed – from deer to rabbits via pheasants, badgers and hedgehogs.

The practicality of collecting road kill is a major stumbling block. Most of these 'pavement pizzas' come a cropper on busy roads in built-up areas and by the time you've got hold of the remains, there's not much usable meat to be had. Country lanes are a less frequent source of road kill, but the meat is likely to be in a much better state.

The main safety concern regarding road kill is cooking. The meat should be very well cooked, ideally slow cooked in a casserole over some hours to tenderise tough meat. Always check the carcass for structural damage. If bones have shattered on impact, they can render the meat almost useless. It should go without saying that meat which doesn't look or smell fresh must always be avoided.

ADVANTAGES: Meat is very expensive, and cars are everywhere. Road kill is a natural way of taking positives from both situations. Wild animal meat tastes as good as free range.

DISADVANTAGES: Beyond the possible health risks mentioned above there is also a certain stigma attached to the idea of shovelling your dinner off the A412, no matter how cheap it is.

INITIAL/ONGOING OUTLAY: none

POTENTIAL SAVING: anything from £500-£1,000 per year.

FREEDOM LIVING SCORE: 8 out of 10

22 KEEP PRODUCTIVE LIVESTOCK

Keeping animals for your own meat, leather, milk, wool or eggs, or simply for company on those long winter nights, takes you to a whole new level of freedom living. We're now firmly in the realms of the self-sufficient and that means having plenty of space and time to look after the animal(s) in question while ensuring you meet the increasingly lengthy list of obligations imposed by the government regarding the ownership and care of livestock.

If you're still keen then you're a better person than I am, so to reward your commitment, here's a brief guide to the most common small-scale livestock options. For the sake of brevity I'm omitting cows, sheep and pigs as they belong on smallholdings, not in back gardens.

GOATS. OK, so goats belong on smallholdings too, but many people mistakenly believe that you can keep a goat on a small patch of grass and it will act as an effective lawnmower and waste disposal unit while recycling all your lush greenery into delicious milk. In reality goats are inefficient mowers, as they prefer rougher, fibrous food and a varied diet. They may eat some grass, but they are just as likely to completely turn their noses up at the prospect. Goats should never be tethered, they should have freedom to roam in a fairly large paddock with decent stock fencing – they should also have shelter and access to fresh water at all times. The milk is delicious, though, as is the meat.

GEESE AND DUCKS. As lawnmowers, geese are a better bet than goats but they can be awfully temperamental. Ducks are generally more even-tempered and they'll do a bit of weeding if the mood takes them, but both varieties of fowl will produce copious amounts of dung that will need clearing up regularly if you don't want to offend your neighbours. On the upside, both produce eggs fairly regularly under the right circumstances and their meat is delicious. As with all fowl, geese and ducks will need access to a free-flowing water source as well as fencing to protect them from predators and a shelter to sleep in at night.

CHICKENS. The most common domestic 'producing' beast, the chicken is also, in my experience, a vicious little monster, although less susceptible to fits of rage than the goose. Chickens are obviously a good source of eggs and versatile meat. They are happy to eat a combination of greens and grain and they're never happier than when they are scratching about for their own food. Consequently you'll need to allow a sizeable area for exercise that doesn't need to be kept pristine. Predators are a risk again, so protective fencing is a must, particularly around the coop.

ADVANTAGES: Eggs, milk and meat are expensive commodities and buying free range or locally sourced produce is sometimes hard. So there's no better feeling than the knowledge that your meat is home-grown.

DISADVANTAGES: Keeping any animals is hard work, not just in daily feeding and maintenance but also in regular mucking-out, collecting eggs, milking and ultimately taking the animal to be killed at a slaughterhouse (and paying for the privilege). Don't try this at home unless you've got serious time and dedication on your side.

INITIAL OUTLAY: cost of goat approx £50-£300, cost of ducklings/goslings/chicks £5 each, food troughs and fresh water supply £25-£50, shelter and vets bills from £100- £1,000.

ONGOING OUTLAY: Food approx £10 per month.

POTENTIAL SAVING: anything from £500-£1,000 per year.

FREEDOM LIVING SCORE: 6 out of 10

23 THE AVIARY AND THE APIARY

If you've taken a look at the prospect of animal husbandry and can't find anything to suit, don't give up just yet. There are two further options that are suitable for anyone's circumstances – from small-scale residential properties to big country houses. They are relatively low maintenance and low stress. Let me tell you about the birds and the bees.

QUAILS. The birds in this case are quails, small and quite beautiful fowl which have several major advantages over other, larger breeds. First of all, they are happy in a relatively small space – half a dozen quail will live quite happily on the floor of an aviary (if you already keep fancy birds) or in their own high-sided coop. The cage needs high sides because quail can actually fly, especially when disturbed, and will damage themselves in a low-roofed environment.

While quails have the propensity to produce muck in quantities that seem disproportionate to their tiny stature, they are otherwise easy to keep. Like chickens they like to scratch and bathe in the dust, but they are not fussy eaters – which is why they suit an aviary so well, as they will survive on a combination of chick crumb and the seeds dropped by other birds.

The major plus point of quails is that in the right conditions and in good light they will produce eggs prolifically – sometimes as often as one egg every eight hours. Quails' eggs are known as a delicacy, but they are equally useful as a substitute for hens' eggs in everyday cooking.

BEES. The buzzing half of this logical equation isn't so easy to establish, but once they are in situ, you'll have a regular little honey factory throbbing away on your behalf for minimal outlay and effort. If you're serious about beekeeping it makes sense to enrol on a course for beginners before you start, or at least contact your local beekeeping society for advice and recommendations of where you can buy a hive and how you can get hold of your first swarm. It is theoretically possible to make your own hive – after all, bees create their own natural 'hives' in the wild – but for ease of access and maintenance there's nothing to beat the traditional wooden hive.

Once a swarm is established you'll have maintenance responsibilities and, of course, honey collection duties, but otherwise the bees are tremendously self-supporting. For honey collecting you'll need the right protective equipment and a decent smoker to subdue the bees while you nick their precious honey. Don't forget that a bonus by-product of the honey-making process is beeswax, which can be formed into candles and used as a furniture polish.

ADVANTAGES: Both quails and bees are natural scavengers, turning natural resources like nectar and dropped seeds into something practical for you: eggs and honey respectively. They're cheap, low maintenance and interesting too.

DISADVANTAGES: There's little meat on a quail, even a well-fed one, so they're not much of a source of food beyond egg production. They can be flighty and they can stop laying if they're disturbed or their environment is too dark. And bees can sting you, of course.

INITIAL OUTLAY: Quails approx £2-£5 each, water supply £5, bee-keeping kit from £50 second-hand to £150-£200+.

ONGOING OUTLAY: £2 a month for quail food, minimal ongoing costs for beekeeping.

POTENTIAL SAVING: Assuming you substitute quails' eggs for hens' eggs in all your cooking and honey for all sugar, you could save around £150-£200 per year.

FREEDOM LIVING SCORE: 9 out of 10

SECTION THREE

HOUSEHOLD BILLS

24 CUT YOUR FUEL COSTS BY CONSERVING ENERGY

Heat and power are major costs, and anyone dedicated to freedom living must work hard to minimise the inefficient and costly waste of energy. This isn't simply good news for the wallet, it's essential for the survival of the planet. So before we move on to the wonderful world of generating alternative energy (see below) we need to focus on the greater and more pressing challenge of energy conservation.

Experts at the Centre for Alternative Technology [see www.cat.org.uk], based in Mid Wales, believe that it is possible to slice up to 80 per cent from heating bills with effective conservation. There are many areas of conservation that will make an immediate impact on household bills, including lifestyle changes such as closing curtains, keeping lids on saucepans, only boiling sufficient water for immediate needs, wearing a jumper; insulating your loft, walls and floor; draught-proofing; installing double glazing (or even triple glazing); using more effective heating controls and thermostats; buying energy efficient appliances and turning off appliances rather than leaving them on standby.

Firstly, ensure you choose energy efficient appliances like condensing gas boilers, which run at 90 per cent efficiency compared with traditional boilers, which come in at a pathetic 65 per cent. Secondly, switch every electrical appliance off at the wall, never leave them on standby or in sleep mode. The average home spends £38 per year on electrical items left on standby mode – this wasteful consumption is known as a 'phantom load', and is common in most appliances, such as DVD players, stereos and TVs. Switching off at the wall is the only way to combat this waste.

Finally, insulate your loft to a CAT recommended maximum thickness of 450mm (government guidelines are currently set at 250mm). You can make an average £180-£220 per year saving on household bills by lining an uninsulated loft with 270mm of insulation.

Until you've achieved these aims, there's no point trying to generate your own energy, as the inefficient waste of power will negate any potential cost benefits.

Insulation and other energy-saving tools are often available free to people on low incomes or offered with hefty government subsidies. The Warm Wales scheme is just one of the examples of government- and industry-led initiatives that aim to equip homes with low-energy light bulbs (another great conservation idea) and other cost-saving benefits. Visit the government's energy efficiency website at www.est.org.uk for more information.

ADVANTAGES: Insulating your house and cutting wasteful energy consumption is a no-brainer. Just do it.

DISADVANTAGES: There are none. Get the picture?

INITIAL OUTLAY: cost of insulation material, depending on the size of your loft space. Cost of buying energy-efficient electrical items and boiler (though there are grants available for boilers).

ONGOING OUTLAY: none

POTENTIAL SAVING: Add all the benefits outlined above together and you'll produce an annual heating bill reduction of at least £300 per year.

FREEDOM LIVING SCORE: 8 out of 10

25 CUT YOUR HEATING COSTS BY GOING VICTORIAN

If you're really serious about cutting the cost of heating your house, you could do a lot worse than following the example of our Victorian forbears, who had to cope with the unfortunate consequences of building houses with massive, high-ceilinged rooms. By the time our grandiose ancestors had cottoned on to the idea that hot air rises, they were freezing their whiskers off.

But undeterred by this, they championed a whole series of draught-proofing measures, like excluders under doors, nightcaps (material, not alcoholic), thick lined curtains at windows and on four-poster beds and even the classic wing-backed chair. All of these functional accoutrements are great and sorely under-utilised methods of performing the simple function of keeping the heat where you need it.

ADVANTAGES: You feel as cosy as a Sunday night costume drama.

DISADVANTAGES: Your house looks like something out of a Sunday night costume drama.

INITIAL OUTLAY: minimal. Old blankets work well as window coverings and draught excluders. Wing-backed chairs can be picked up for £30-£40 at a junk shop.

ONGOING OUTLAY: none

POTENTIAL SAVING: as with all insulation, the savings are considerable – anything from £30-£80 per year.

FREEDOM LIVING SCORE: 7 out of 10

26 SWITCH TO WOOD BURNERS

If your idea of burning wood in the home involves a pretty little pile of logs spitting and crackling in the grate, please look away now. What we're dealing with here is the serious business of burning wood for maximum effect – that means acquiring whatever wood you can find, gather and scavenge in whatever form. Barn-dried logs are all very well, but at £5 per small net bag, they're the most expensive way to use wood as fuel.

Step one of converting to wood burners is to select the right stove for your requirements. The size of the stove will depend on the amount of heat you need to generate and whether you intend to use it with a back boiler for heating your domestic water and/or radiators as well. Multi-fuel stoves tend to have small fireboxes and consequently burn fuel inefficiently. Old-fashioned Rayburn or Aga stoves that are used for cooking and as a heating and hot water source, are also fairly inefficient as the demands on one appliance to fulfil all three tasks are excessive. Smaller scale wood burners are sometimes adaptable for water heating as well. Don't be tempted to buy a huge wood burner for a small space. They are very efficient and you'll be wasting money if you have to keep the windows open because you're overheating your room. For an average 15ftx15ft room, the smallest stoves are more than adequate, though again if you're heating water you may need a larger size.

It isn't necessary to buy new – take a look around reclamation yards, where you'll usually find a wide selection of stoves in varying states of decay. Most are salvageable and just need a coat of stove blacking. If you must buy new, source your stove direct from the manufacturer or wholesaler – check prices on trading websites like eBay for the best deals.

For safety and efficiency's sakes, you should always install your wood burner with a properly fitted flue. If you've got a large chimney or inglenook make sure you have a good fireproof register plate fitted – this is the sheet of material that blocks off the chimney cavity. The flue pipe passes through a hole in the register plate, but the heat from the burner isn't wasted heating the chimney cavity.

As regards wood, there are many cheap sources of burning material, as long as you don't mind what it looks like. Furniture manufacturers, timber yards and demolition sites often have off-cuts and surplus timber lying about and are happy for you to remove it for free. Never burn wood that's been painted or treated with a substance that's likely to give off poisonous fumes.

There's not much money to be made from selling logs – even farm gate operations aren't particularly profitable – so you may also find that a farmer or landowner with a lot of surplus wood will be happy to negotiate a hefty discount if you'll remove wood in bulk. It might pay to invest in your own log splitter or chainsaw, as that way you can offer to help cut down problem trees for your neighbours, taking away the remnants in part payment. Never be ashamed of picking up fallen branches when you're out and about in the countryside – they make excellent kindling.

ADVANTAGES: Burning wood is the oldest form of heating and just about the easiest. If your stove is properly installed and sealed, it's also highly efficient.

DISADVANTAGES: Sourcing wood can be a problem in built-up areas. Storage is also a major issue, as the wood needs to be kept dry where possible.

INITIAL OUTLAY: depending on need, a wood burner can cost anything from £150-£1,500. Range cookers are more expensive. The flue and fittings can set you back a further £500, but if you can source your wood cheap you'll earn this outlay back in no time.

ONGOING OUTLAY: cost of wood and chimney sweeping (at £50 a go, twice a year)

POTENTIAL SAVING: an efficient system that provides all the heat and hot water you need could save around £500 a year, while generating 74 per cent of all the energy you need in the home.

FREEDOM LIVING SCORE: 9 out of 10

27 HEAT YOUR HOUSEHOLD WATER USING SOLAR GAIN

There are two main ways to harness the power of the sun – solar water heating and photo-voltaic panels (more commonly called solar panels) which generate electricity. We'll come back to the latter, more costly method later, but first we'll look at ways to generate hot water only.

The first thing to say is that in the UK you're unlikely to be able to rely on the sun to provide your hot water requirements all year. In the winter months, you will need a back-up, which is why CAT recommends a system that combines wood burners with solar heating.

The most efficient way to generate hot water from the power of the sun is by fitting an evacuated tube system to your roof. These use a low volume of water over a small surface area (approximately $3m^2$ is sufficient to heat the water used by an average sized house). Another popular system is the flat plate collector, which uses a system of insulated black pipes. This is not so efficient, requiring a surface area of 4 sq m to heat sufficient water.

These systems will cost approximately £2,500 installed and fitted. It is possible to buy them as kits and install them yourself, but the cost saving doesn't really offset the hassle of scrabbling around on your roof. There are grants available from the DTI to offset some of the cost of installing these systems.

If you're determined to follow the freedom living principle to the letter and you've got some plumbing experience, you can reproduce some of the benefits of solar heating systems by painting old radiators black, attaching them to your roof and connecting them to the water supply. Obviously, as these aren't designed for the purpose and the volume of water carried is great they are much less efficient than the other methods outlined above. But it does have the advantage that you can pick up the materials for a song from a salvage yard.

ADVANTAGES: As part of an overall system, solar water heating is a low-impact and effective back-up. It'll put an even bigger smile on your face when the sun shines.

DISADVANTAGES: Some people feel the pipes/tubes/radiators look unsightly and the resulting heat generation can be intermittent and disappointing. A bit like the British summer.

INITIAL OUTLAY: £2,500 installed

ONGOING OUTLAY: none

POTENTIAL SAVING: A quarter of our energy use is water heating, so a family house with a £500 heating bill could save around £60 per year and get about 50 per cent of the annual hot water requirements from solar water heating.

FREEDOM LIVING SCORE: 8 out of 10

28 GENERATE YOUR OWN HOUSEHOLD SOLAR POWER

Photovoltaic panels convert the power of the sun into electricity. They are very costly to install – even with a government grant – but are efficient to use and an excellent method of powering small, infrequent use items (which is why they are often seen powering illuminated road signs, for example).

As a principal source of power generation in a domestic environment in the UK they aren't likely to prove terribly cost effective at current prices and don't offer the same year-round reliability as other alternative energy sources. If your house is in the right location, with a roof that faces south without obstructions from buildings or trees, you may even be able to generate sufficient energy to sell some back to the National Grid. If your house isn't connected to the mains, photovoltaic panels are an excellent alternative, though even in this case it is virtually impossible to live on power generated by photovoltaic panels alone because they simply don't get enough sun in winter. Off-grid energy generation usually requires a combination of solar panels and another source, such as wind.

ADVANTAGES: Another reasonably efficient way to convert the sun's power to energy.

DISADVANTAGES: High cost means a very long pay back time.

INITIAL OUTLAY: Systems range in price but an average system can be installed for around £15,000. Government grants were available to cover half the cost of this, but these have recently been capped at £2,500.

ONGOING OUTLAY: none

POTENTIAL SAVING: Savings are difficult to calculate as they are dependent on location and tariff. In the right environment they could save around £240 a year, rising to a potential profit in sales back to the National Grid. Across the UK, the saving is likely to be closer to an average of £120 per year.

FREEDOM LIVING SCORE: 6 out of 10

29 GENERATE YOUR OWN HOUSEHOLD WIND POWER

The old estate agents' mantra 'location, location, location' is never more accurate than when applied to renewable energy sources. As with photovoltaic panels, wind turbines are only truly cost-effective in the right circumstances. If your property is on a hill, with an even and steady wind and with no obstructions like trees or buildings, then a wind turbine may well work for you.

If you're a skilled metalworker you can build your own, providing you also have the technical know-how to connect it to a battery for storage. You're better off buying a ready-assembled turbine for a few thousand pounds.

Wind power is a matter of feast and famine. In a gale, you cannot hope to harness and store the power of the wind, and when it is calm, there's barely enough energy generated to power a small bulb. Consequently, wind power generation on a small scale (as opposed to the giant offshore wind farms around the coast and on bleak moors across the country) is most likely to be feasible as a back-up source of energy only, and could only be considered as the main source of energy for heating a house or a hot water system if you're using a large and expensive turbine along with enough battery power to cope with calm days and/or combining this system with photovoltaic panels.

ADVANTAGES: If you're in the right part of the world, a wind turbine will support your renewable energy system. At least if you're somewhere that doesn't get much sun, the chances are you'll get plenty of wind.

DISADVANTAGES: There are few tangible benefits of small-scale wind power generation in isolation.

INITIAL OUTLAY: wind turbines can cost from £500 to £10,000 depending on size and purpose. At the low end of this scale, the turbine would power a few lights; at the high end, a turbine sited in a good location would power an entire house.

ONGOING OUTLAY: none

POTENTIAL SAVING: £0-£1,020 per year, depending on location and existing tariff. The pay back time is long.

FREEDOM LIVING SCORE: 5 out of 10

30 GENERATE YOUR OWN HOUSEHOLD HYDROELECTRIC POWER

A water source is another potential avenue of energy generation. Again, much depends on the location of your water source. To stand a realistic chance of cost-effective generation you need a combination of factors, namely a fast flowing stream and a good vertical drop. There is a simple calculation to give you a rough idea of the power (in watts) that you can expect to generate from a given water source, which is as follows:

Flow (in litres per second) × Head Height (vertical drop in metres) × 10 (the specific weight of water) ÷ 2 = the power generated.

On a small scale, the most cost-effective turbine is the Pelton Wheel and these require a vertical drop of at least 10 metres.

If you've got this facility available to you, use it. If not, forget it, as you won't be able to make cost-effective use of your water source.

ADVANTAGES: In the right conditions, hydroelectric power is a stable and steady power source.

DISADVANTAGES: The right conditions are hard to find and almost impossible to recreate.

INITIAL OUTLAY: cost of setting up the turbine and power storage = £11,000+, although hydroelectricity costs are very site-specific.

ONGOING OUTLAY: none

POTENTIAL SAVING: £1,000 per year

FREEDOM LIVING SCORE: 7 out of 10

31 SAVE YOUR COMPOST AND WASTE

There is one further power generation method worth mentioning in passing. It's possible to extract gas from human and animal waste to make fuel. While it might seem like a bridge too far for all but the most dedicated eco-warrior, there is an untapped reservoir of power stored up in our dung and kitchen waste which is just waiting to be let out.

So why don't we exploit it more? Well we do, but only on a grand commercial scale at sewage treatment plants. While humans and animals (especially pigs, naturally) have the capacity to produce methane gas and we have the technology to extract and store it, no one has yet made this process viable for the small-scale market as the heat loss is too great on a small scale due to the ratio of volume to surface area. So since we're dealing only with processes that have the capacity to save money, we must discount small-scale gas generation. In other parts of the world, where the climate is more favourable, like India for example, gas from dung is often used as a fuel. But sadly it remains a distant dream in the UK for now.

Never fear, however, as there are other uses for your waste – a compost bin built from a couple of larch lap fence panels is the perfect store for kitchen waste that can be rotted down as a general purpose compost. A composting toilet is a great way to compost human dung which produces the most incredible garden fertiliser – though this should only ever be used around plants and should never come into contact with foodstuffs.

ADVANTAGES: Human and animal waste produces wonderful plant food.

DISADVANTAGES: Getting in touch with nature is fine, but rooting around in your family's dung is a step too far for some of us.

INITIAL/ONGOING OUTLAY: no outlay for composting, £150-£200 to build a basic composting toilet facility.

POTENTIAL SAVING: a composting toilet saves on fertiliser and water usage, to the tune of £50-£100 per year.

FREEDOM LIVING SCORE: 8 out of 10

32 CREATE A 'GREY WATER' REUSE SYSTEM IN YOUR HOUSE

The basic principle behind saving money on water consumption is the same as that for energy consumption – conserve rather than reuse. Commit to fixing dripping taps, take showers rather than baths, put a litre plastic bottle filled with water or a cistern displacement device that is freely available from your water authority in your toilet cistern (never use a brick as these can disintegrate and the particles may cause damage to the toilet), only flush for solid waste, don't let the tap run while cleaning your teeth. All of these tips will cut your water use. If you have a water meter, you'll see the tangible benefits of these measures immediately. And if you haven't got a water meter, ask your water supplier to fit one.

It is possible to reuse water, but with some specific guidelines. Water used in a house takes two essential forms: black water and grey water. Black water is specifically that which has been flushed down the toilet. This water must never be reused. Grey water is the water that is used in the sink, shower or bath and in the washing machine or washing up, in cooking and preparing food. It may contain detergents and will also contain bacteria. Because these bacteria multiply at a frantic rate, grey water must never be stored, but it can be used to irrigate crops and plants. It is theoretically possible to clean grey water using a small-scale filtration and treatment plant, but for domestic use this is neither cost-effective nor energy-efficient.

The simplest way to incorporate a grey water irrigation system into your house is to fit a diverter to the down pipe from the bath or shower. The grey water should then be fed via a system of pipes directly into the plant or vegetable beds. At the Centre for Alternative Technology there is a grey water irrigation system on display which feeds into raised vegetable beds through perforated pipes.

While grey water is generally safe for irrigation purposes, it's worth remembering that the run-off from the washing machine in particular may have quite a high salt content, and so this grey water may have a negative effect if applied to the same area of the garden for too long. It's good practice to spread the watering around as much as possible.

ADVANTAGES: The grey water system is very logical. In the spring and summer we need to shower and bathe more frequently and our plants and vegetables need more moisture. It makes perfect sense to be able to combine these demands on water consumption to our mutual benefit.

DISADVANTAGES: The irrigation system may require a bit of plumbing know-how.

INITIAL OUTLAY: the cost of fitting the diverter (£20-£27) and irrigation system (an old hose pipe, a sink and some plastic piping will suffice).

ONGOING OUTLAY: none

POTENTIAL SAVING: depending on your normal water consumption this could save £40 per year.

FREEDOM LIVING SCORE: 9 out of 10.

33 COLLECT RAINWATER FOR DOMESTIC AND GARDEN USE

Another way to cut consumption of fresh water is to ensure you maximise your use of one of the UK's most abundant natural resources – the rain.

Rainwater is generally cleaner than grey water, though it may also include bacteria from a range of sources – from dead animals in your gutter to pollution from the atmosphere. However, you can save rainwater in butts for some time and reuse this water on the garden. It's also perfectly good for washing the car.

Because rainwater is generally fairly clean, it's also possible to reuse it in the house if you fit a simple sieve-like filter to your down pipes. Once it has been filtered it is perfectly useful as water for the toilet, or even for use in the washing machine.

ADVANTAGES: It's plentiful and free.

DISADVANTAGES: The rain doesn't tend to fall when it's needed most, so you will need to plan an appropriate-sized system of water storage. You'll also need to practise some water-efficient gardening.

INITIAL OUTLAY: the cost of water butts, approximately £25. Some local authorities offer special cut-price water butts to their residents.

ONGOING OUTLAY: none

POTENTIAL SAVING: £12 per year

FREEDOM LIVING SCORE: 9 out of 10

34 'PLAY THE MARKET' WITH ELECTRICITY AND GAS SUPPLIERS

Ever since the energy supply market was opened up, there have been rival companies fighting for our attention, offering great deals, fixed term offers and even free gifts to get us on board.

Along with the proliferation of energy supply companies, there's been a notable increase in price-comparison websites, most notably Uswitch.com, which offer a realistic comparison of the deals offered by the various main players in the market. Although there's no such thing as a completely disinterested comparison site, they are useful to use as a broad benchmark for what's available.

Switching supplier regularly poses more problems logistically than financially, as the administration of such transfers can sometimes become quite complex, involving a lot of time on the phone sorting things out and negating any real benefit of switching, as your chosen supplier will inevitably have to raise their own prices in the end to remain competitive.

The most sensible reason to switch is if you are offered a decent locked-in deal for a fixed period of time. Energy prices are on the up, and they aren't about to decline any time soon, so if you get the chance to cap your price, you're well advised to take it.

ADVANTAGES: If you've never switched electricity or gas supplier, you're almost certainly getting a raw deal, because someone, somewhere will offer you a better deal to secure your custom.

DISADVANTAGES: If you don't choose wisely, or if you swap too frequently, you'll end up paying more in the end.

INITIAL/ONGOING OUTLAY: zero for swapping.

POTENTIAL SAVING: depending on the offer, anything up to £100-150 per year, but if you're offered a good capped deal, think of it as a long-term benefit.

FREEDOM LIVING SCORE: 5 out of 10

35 USE INTERNET PHONE SERVICES FOR FREE NATIONAL AND INTERNATIONAL CALLS

One of the greatest revolutions brought about by high speed internet access is the free VOIP (Voice Over Internet Protocol) call. The most famous global example of this is Skype, an offshoot of eBay, while many people across the globe also communicate using Windows Live Messenger. Providing you and the person you're talking to are both sitting in front of your PCs, are connected to the internet via high speed broadband link and have headphones or a handset connected to your computer, you can make a call from one side of the world to the other without paying a penny for the privilege.

If you've got a lot of family spread out around the globe, the benefits of this are enormous, but Skype in particular is useful for a much wider range of applications – you can effectively use it as a second phone line as it can be used while the landline is busy. But remember that the only free calls are Skype to Skype, all other types of call will cost you, but additional services are available to subscribers.

ADVANTAGES: If you make a lot of international calls, you'll see the immediate benefits on your phone bill. Despite a shaky start, the technology is now pretty sophisticated and clear-sounding.

DISADVANTAGES: Your cousin in Sydney may object to getting up in the middle of the night just to save you a few quid on calls.

INITIAL OUTLAY: a Skype headset (for example) can cost as little as £15. Everything else is free (except for the computer and the broadband)

ONGOING OUTLAY: for Skype to Skype calls, none.

POTENTIAL SAVING: £50-£100+ per year.

FREEDOM LIVING SCORE: 8 out of 10

36 GET FREE TV AND AXE YOUR LICENCE FEE

If you don't own a TV or any device capable of receiving a TV signal, you don't need a TV licence. But doesn't that mean you can't ever watch TV programmes? Not any more. The BBC and Channel 4 have both introduced web-based services for accessing content at a time that suits you.

With the BBC iPlayer [www.bbc.co.uk/iplayer/] you can watch BBC shows after they've happened, although you will need a decent, high-speed broadband connection. Channel 4's on-demand service works in a similar way, although some content is subscription only. In addition to saving you money, these services suit a more flexible lifestyle, rather than being chained to the regular TV schedule. Expect other broadcasters to follow suit – it's the future.

ADVANTAGES: No more missed shows, no repeats, no adverts. It's also great for kids who want to watch shows again and again.

DISADVANTAGES: Not a great viewing experience for anyone who is used to a 40-inch screen and computers often have poor sound quality. Avoiding a TV licence in this way isn't illegal but it's not very communitarian either. Both services are only available to internet users in the UK..

INITIAL/ONGOING OUTLAY: none at present, but expect subscription services to begin soon.

POTENTIAL SAVING: £135.50 per year

FREEDOM LIVING SCORE: 5 out of 10

37 MAKE SURE YOU'RE GETTING THE BENEFITS YOU QUALIFY FOR

There's a fine line between freeloading and getting what you deserve, and for fear of crossing from the latter to the former, many people don't question whether they could be entitled to more government help to supplement their income.

Government support for low-income living is a complex area and depends on individual circumstances, but it is always worth your while asking whether you're entitled to any extra help, both in terms of day-to-day living and with specific events, like giving birth (do you qualify for a Sure Start Maternity Grant?) and entering higher education (do you qualify for a bursary towards your tuition fees?).

One of the best, free places to go for independent advice on your financial well-being is the Citizens Advice Bureau [www.citizensadvice.org.uk] which has branches all over the UK staffed by people who can offer real support and guidance to ensure you're getting everything you deserve.

ADVANTAGES: It's another case of 'if you don't ask, you don't get'. Bursaries and grants are provided for specific purposes, and there's no shame in claiming what's rightly yours.

DISADVANTAGES: Minimal. Some application processes are complex.

INITIAL/ONGOING OUTLAY: none

POTENTIAL SAVING: dependent on circumstances, but possibly £1,000 or more.

FREEDOM LIVING SCORE: 6 out of 10

38 SUPERMARKET LOYALTY CARDS – HOW TO GET THE BEST FROM THEM

Although anyone dedicated to living for free might be forgiven for avoiding supermarkets like the plague, there are some great deals to be had courtesy of certain stores' loyalty schemes. There are three main loyalty cards available: Sainsbury's Nectar card, Tesco

Clubcard and Boots Advantage card. Waterstone's has also introduced a loyalty card for customers, though the benefits are currently limited.

Tesco and Sainsbury's seem to have cornered the market in effective loyalty card administration, mainly by extending their network of associated point-gathering retailers – from car hire firms to restaurants and most trades in between. Nectar and Clubcard points are also used in-store as effective promotion tools. If either retailer wants to promote a new product or service, they often sweeten the pill with a giant points bonus. On a DVD club promotion, for example, Tesco offered 1000 points (£10) to anyone who signed up to their club for a minimum of three months. With a basic monthly fee of £4.47 a month, this meant access to free DVDs for three months for less than a fiver. A good deal.

It's also worth checking for double and treble points deals on specific products. Some of these deals are only available via promotional coupons that you receive with your points statement, so cross-check them carefully to make sure you get the most from your spending.

The final, crucial piece of advice is to check out the dedicated points website for each of the retailers mentioned above. These sites have details of the reward deals on offer to cardholders, which are often better value than simply redeeming your points in store. Again using Tesco as an example, each point is awarded for a pound spent and is worth a penny in store, but it is tripled if redeemed against a voucher obtained via the Clubcard website to be used in selected restaurants, thus turning a £10 Clubcard voucher into a £30 meal ticket. Similar deals are offered on magazine subscriptions and other products and services.

ADVANTAGES: The cards come for free, so if you're spending the money anyway, why not reap the benefits?

DISADVANTAGES: Some people become obsessed with points deals, buying a hundredweight of bananas just because they're on triple points. Try to strike a balance between getting a great deal and keeping a grip on reality.

INITIAL/ONGOING OUTLAY: none

POTENTIAL SAVING: If you maximise your points by getting rewards vouchers, you can save the price of a family meal out each month.

FREEDOM LIVING SCORE: 6 out of 10

39 TAKE ADVANTAGE OF FREE CREDIT ON STORE AND CREDIT CARDS

The credit crunch makes life hard for all of us, but anyone wanting to live for free should seriously dedicate themselves to eradicating their debts. Holding credit cards and store cards that are carrying debt at high monthly interest charges makes no sense whatsoever. Without wishing to sound like an awful daytime TV advert, you need to consolidate and rationalise.

Rationalising your finances is discussed below, but here we need to look at ways to use credit facilities to your advantage. Once you've achieved this, and have successfully cleared your card balance, I'd recommend putting the credit card away for emergencies only.

Interest-free credit and interest-free balance transfers are limited time offers that can help you clear credit card debt. Check the small print of any balance transfer deal, as most include an administration charge. As long as the new card's deal is entirely free, you have a matter of months to clear the balance without incurring interest. If you can't find a good balance transfer deal and still need to clear existing balances, prioritise your payments according to the size of the interest rate. You'll still be paying interest, but at least it won't be top whack.

Finally, before you consider switching to another card, ring your current card company and tell them you're going to jump ship. They'll almost certainly offer you a better deal than the one you're current on if you agree to stay loyal. That might save you the hassle of switching, and a few quid into the bargain.

ADVANTAGES: Credit card companies are extremely competitive, and that's still good news for customers. Check out a price comparison website for a more detailed breakdown of what's on offer.

DISADVANTAGES: If you put anything on credit card, it means you're spending money you haven't got. As a rule, that's a bad habit to get into.

INITIAL/ONGOING OUTLAY: none

POTENTIAL SAVING: this depends on your outstanding balance and the size of your interest payments.

FREEDOM LIVING SCORE: 5 out of 10

40 MAKE SURE YOUR MONEY IS WORKING FOR YOU

Even if you're incredibly sensible with your money and never find yourself in debt that still doesn't mean you're working the system to maximum advantage. Here are some quick tips to make sure your cash is working hard for you:

TAX FREE SAVINGS. If you've got the wherewithal to save some money, make sure you take advantage of cash ISA savings. These are safe, long-term savings accounts that pay a decent rate of tax-free interest.

SELF-ASSESSMENT PAYS. If you're self-employed or are a PAYE employee with other sources of income you'll be required to fill in a self-assessment tax return. This small annual inconvenience can be a massive financial advantage. If you can find yourself a good, cheap accountant, they can advise you on what is and isn't tax deductible. You'll be surprised at just how much you can claim for and what a difference this can make to your annual tax bill.

BE PREPARED. This isn't exactly a money-saving tip, more like a good housekeeping move. Many financial services providers offer good rates of interest on savings accounts providing you open the account with a decent lump sum of money (for example £500). If you can afford to squirrel away this kind of cash you can regard it as a contingency fund, available in an emergency, or to fund big costs like car insurance or tax bills. All the while it's tucked away, it is earning you money, and it saves you from hitting the credit card.

ADVANTAGES: Being smart with your money makes you money and saves you on interest charges and debt.

DISADVANTAGES: High interest accounts sometimes make it hard to access your cash in a hurry.

INITIAL/ONGOING OUTLAY: none

POTENTIAL SAVING: a few thousand pounds saved in an ISA, for example, could be earning you a couple of hundred pounds a year for nothing.

FREEDOM LIVING SCORE: 7 out of 10

41 BE DEMANDING AND WRITE TO COMPLAIN ABOUT POOR SERVICE – GET WHAT YOU WANT OR GET YOUR MONEY BACK

Despite being labelled with a 'mustn't grumble' attitude, we're actually quite effective complainers in the UK. We vote with our feet, and when a service or product hasn't come up to our standards, we'll politely return or refuse it, then walk away and badmouth the offending company to all and sundry.

For this reason, it always pays to contact the company concerned and explain in cool, collected language exactly why they have incurred your displeasure. There's no point in ranting down the phone to the store or tearing a strip off a pimply sales assistant. Even if they are to blame, they don't have the power or the sense to do anything about it.

Instead, get out your best notepaper and compose a letter to the head office customer services department, explaining exactly what happened and how much it has upset you. This letter is the company's lifeline as you are likely to delay your badmouthing until they have responded.

Most companies with any clout or ambition will seize this opportunity to make up for the problem by offering you a satisfactory solution that gives you a better deal than you'd have had in the first place. They avoid a tongue-lashing and you leave with what you wanted, only cheaper/better/twice as much. Whoever said that complaining didn't make people happy?

ADVANTAGES: It puts the customer in their rightful place, at the top of the heap.

DISADVANTAGES: You'll inevitably come across a company that wants to argue the toss, which will cost you stress and time.

INITIAL/ONGOING OUTLAY: minimal

POTENTIAL SAVING: depends on the original product/service

FREEDOM LIVING SCORE: 7 out of 10 (including a point for consumer rights)

42 HOW TO RUN YOUR CAR FROM VEGETABLE OIL

Anyone who's watched the price of fuel creep up to and beyond the £1 per litre mark will have taken an interest in the gathering pace of the biodiesel revolution. Reports in the media give conflicting accounts of the potential damaging effects of biodiesel on an engine, but no one is disputing the fact that a car run on biodiesel is a whole load cheaper than one that takes conventional fuel.

Converting your car to run on biodiesel isn't an easy process and it certainly can't be achieved for free, but the cost of the equipment involved can be quickly and easily offset by savings made on fuel. After a few months of motoring, you'll find yourself sitting on a goldmine.

Patrick Whetman of Goat Industries has been producing biodiesel and vegetable oil conversion kits since the fuel blockade in 2001 threatened the supply of fuel for consumer use. Patrick's firm was the first to be set up in response to the fuel crisis and he has become one of the leading advocates of alternative/sustainable fuel technologies in the UK.

"I set up my first biodiesel plant as a project that interested me. It was something for the future," Patrick explains. "At that time, no one else was doing it – I made a lot of mistakes in the early days, as you never really know how to master the skill until you try it out."

In the relatively short time that Patrick has been producing fuel and supplying equipment for others to do likewise, he's found that demand for fuel – from obvious sources such as chip shops and school kitchens – has increased significantly, while the price of oil has risen accordingly, and has more than doubled in recent years. "There's a high demand for oil now and that will only drive prices upward," predicts Patrick.

In spite of this trend, Patrick is still confident that the production of biodiesel is cost effective for anyone trying to cut fuel costs on an individual basis, especially as it is now possible to produce 2,500 litres of biodiesel for personal use without having to pay any tax on the fuel. Yet there are still some serious pitfalls, as Patrick explains:

"Producing your own fuel involves dealing with dangerous chemicals, which brings with it an element of safety risk. There are other considerations, depending on how you plan to generate fuel – if you use a vegetable oil filtration plant, these are generally cheap but have little functionality and are very messy. You will get covered in oil."

So what does Patrick recommend as a starting point for the wannabe biodiesel generator? "It's important to be well organised," he says. "Make an investment in the best machine you can afford. Get a good machine that is cleanable and that's made from heavy grade materials. A decent quality machine will pay for itself in no time and will be virtually indestructible into the bargain."

ADVANTAGES: Halving the cost of motoring is a pretty appealing prospect. There's also an innate feeling of flicking a devil-may-care finger in the direction of the oil barons.

DISADVANTAGES: Smelly, oily and potentially dangerous working conditions mean that this is an activity geared towards the dedicated. You also need a lot of space for the processing plant.

INITIAL OUTLAY: for a decent quality processor look to spend around £1,000.

ONGOING OUTLAY: you will need to pay for oil and chemicals (though you might get the oil free if you can reach a deal with a friendly chippy).

POTENTIAL SAVING: £1,000+ per year

FREEDOM LIVING SCORE: 7 out of 10

43 BECOME A SECURITY GUARDIAN OF A PROPERTY AND LIVE FOR NEXT TO NOTHING

Getting a foot on the property ladder is just about the hardest financial step for any young person. Spiralling mortgage costs have driven up rents as well, and the squeeze on wages means that the gap between what someone can afford and what they actually want is growing ever wider.

But there is an alternative for anyone who wants to reduce the costs of living and who doesn't mind a more sociable and potentially varied living arrangement. Property management firm Camelot has a portfolio of extraordinary properties around the UK and Ireland, which it manages on behalf of the owners. The company finds professionals to live in the properties – which can range from penthouse apartments to warehouses by way of farms, manor houses and castles – and these so-called guardians act as a form of security measure for the empty property. Rents are incredibly low (around a quarter of the average) and also include bills.

There is a downside to all this easy living, as the properties are sometimes only available short-term, although the company tries to give residents a three-month stay as a minimum and a month's notice to quit on top of that. Once you are on Camelot's books, they will also strive to find you alternative accommodation if required. Many guardians find themselves in properties for longer-term stays, and even manage to create a cosy living environment in the unlikeliest places. Check out the firm's website at www.camelotproperty.com

ADVANTAGES: Low rents and communal living make this a great option for young professionals who are keen to live independently but also gather some savings for the step up to home ownership.

DISADVANTAGES: It's an insecure life and the company doesn't have a huge portfolio in the UK at present, so there may not be much choice.

INITIAL OUTLAY: £500 approximately deposit, registration fee and fire safety pack.

ONGOING OUTLAY: £25-£60 per week rent.

POTENTIAL SAVING: huge – anything up to £4,000-£5,000 per year.

FREEDOM LIVING SCORE: 8 out of 10

44 MAKE YOUR OWN SOAPS, MOISTURISERS AND TOILETRIES

It had to happen eventually. The more TV adverts we see featuring women washing their hair in waterfalls surrounded by nature's bounty, the more we get wise to the fact that natural, organic products are actually better for us than the long list of pharmaceutical hybrids that drugs companies try to get us to put on our hair, skin and teeth. They've only got themselves to blame.

If you cling to the mumbo-jumbo experts and desire the latest miracle ingredient to send your skin whizzing back through the decades or give your gappy molars the Julia Roberts treatment, then carry on chucking your money away. The rest of us, however, can take a look in the larder for our beauty tips.

Good quality, pure oils – almond, avocado, coconut and sesame are common examples – can form the basis of a range of skin moisturisers. Blend a few tablespoons of your chosen oils with a little cocoa butter and a tablespoon of beeswax (from your own hive, naturally) to make a useful all-over moisturiser.

Rather than wasting money on expensive toothpaste with a baking soda tingle, just use baking soda instead. Wet your brush and drop some powder onto it, or mix up a special concoction using baking soda and herbs like sage or mint with a drop or two of essential oil.

Baking soda mixed with essential oils also makes a reasonable alternative to talcum powder or deodorant. Sweet smelling oils like rose and lavender are especially good.

The drawback of these natural store-cupboard toiletries is that, like all products, they may produce an allergic reaction – especially the essential oils and nut oils. So test a small, discreet patch of skin with any new concoction, and obviously avoid any oils that you wouldn't otherwise ingest.

ADVANTAGES: You look and smell great, feel virtuous and use up all the ingredients from the cupboard that you've never found a purpose for.

DISADVANTAGES: It can feel a little bit like you're basting yourself. Some pure oils can be almost as expensive as the cosmetics they are replacing, so shop with care.

INITIAL OUTLAY: the basic ingredients for the above toiletries should be around £10.

ONGOING OUTLAY: if kept in dry and/or airtight containers, the products should last months.

POTENTIAL SAVING: £50 per year

FREEDOM LIVING SCORE: 7 out of 10

45 EAT HEALTHY, BE HEALTHY

The above statement might sound as if it's from the 'bleeding obvious' school, but it is worthwhile considering exactly how much time (and consequently money) we lose by feeling ill or sluggish because of our diet. The more healthy food we eat, the more energy we have, and the more energy we have, the more we can do with our days.

It can be pretty demeaning to think of the body as a machine in this way, but that's exactly what it is – if we don't provide it with the right fuel it will conk out somewhere between 5pm and bedtime. Aside from the common advice of drinking a plentiful amount of water (up to two litres) each day and consuming five portions of fruit and vegetables daily and two portions of fish weekly, here are a few key tips to keep you thriving:

SUPERFOOD = SUPERPEOPLE. Make an effort to incorporate so-called 'superfoods' like apricots and cranberries into your diet – sprinkle them on cereals if you can't stomach them alone.

BE VITAMIN RICH. Vitamin C is the oldest cold cure even if it's not the most reliable one, and it's present in many more foods than just the humble orange. Eat strawberries, peppers and green vegetables for a varied Vitamin-C rich diet.

GET ENERGY – SLOWLY. There's no point in getting the kind of quick energy hit that soft drinks and sweets give you. Your energy levels will soar briefly and will plummet soon after. Eat slow-release foods like bananas and wholewheat pasta for a more gradual energy hit that will keep you going longer.

CUT SUGAR AND SALT. These ingredients add little to food, and they make you feel very bad. If you're trying to save money, never buy processed food, which is caked in preservatives, sugar, salt and fat. Prepare everything from scratch, it's more fun, doesn't take anywhere near as long as you think it will and you can control the ingredients you use. If you must add a sweetener, use natural honey.

ADVANTAGES: If you eat smarter, you'll feel better, look better and save money.

DISADVANTAGES: With no more fast food binges, you'll have to find other ways to amuse yourself after a bad day.

INITIAL/ONGOING OUTLAY: prices from a farmers' market or farm shop are comparable to supermarket prices – and quality is far higher. Anyway, you'll be growing it all yourself, won't you?

POTENTIAL SAVING: by switching from processed to natural foods, you can save around £20 a week from your food bill.

FREEDOM LIVING SCORE: 8 out of 10

46 MEND YOUR OWN CAR AND BUY PARTS FROM SALVAGE

If you must have a car – and the dedicated low-cost life would ideally be free of such a money drain – then it's important to avoid excessive garage bills. There are certain unavoidable running costs like insurance, tax and MOT inspections. But beyond these, the money we spend on services, check-ups and other niggling irritations is a downright waste.

The first thing you need to do is get hold of a decent manual for your make of car – Haynes manuals can be picked up for a few pence from boot fairs, or you can get manuals on most popular makes from the library. Your car's user manual will also have some basic information on general maintenance. Get hold of some basic tools, such as a set of spanners, screwdrivers and pliers and try to learn at the very least the basics of a simple car service.

The more proficient you become at car maintenance, the more money you'll save, and if you do encounter any serious problems which require replacement parts, don't go straight to the main dealer for a costly replacement. Breakers' yards are a great source of spare parts, sometimes in excellent condition and at a fraction of the new selling price. Some breakers' yards, like www.metrosalvage.com offer an online parts sourcing service.

Finally, if you do develop a decent level of maintenance skills, it is easier to maintain an older, more basic car than a newer vehicle with a complex electronic engine management system. As long as your chosen car has strong bodywork and a decent history of maintenance and care, you'll be able to keep it on the road yourself for years to come.

ADVANTAGES: Keeping your car out of the garage makes financial sense, but in general terms it pays to be a bit savvy about car maintenance, both to check the signs of problems in your car before they become serious, and to challenge any unscrupulous mechanic who tries to convince you to part with your cash.

DISADVANTAGES: It's a steep learning curve for many of us, especially as cars are becoming more complex. Like them or loathe them, mechanics are also (generally) good at keeping you safe, so if you are going to take on your own maintenance, you must be dedicated to the craft.

INITIAL OUTLAY: for the manual and basic toolkit, £25 to £50.

ONGOING OUTLAY: parts and oil and so on for annual service around £30-£40.

POTENTIAL SAVING: up to £250 per year in servicing and repair costs.

FREEDOM LIVING SCORE: 7 out of 10

47 USE FREE SALVAGE BUILDING MATERIALS/ LANDSCAPING MATERIALS

Where there's muck, there's brass, as grim northern industrialists are fond of observing. That truism is never truer than when it is applied to demolition sites and building projects, where there's often a huge spill of broken up hardcore or topsoil available for removal by anyone who's got the means to take it.

If you're planning your own landscaping project, or building the world's biggest rockery, this material is a priceless commodity. The only problem is how to find and access this kind of stuff. Fortunately, via the wonderful web, potential large-scale scavengers can visit sites like www.SalvoMIE.com and gain access to a whole network of construction site waste that's ready to be picked up. Some firms will even drop off the offending waste for a small fee if you don't have the transport. The types of material available through this kind of site aren't just limited to landscaping materials. There's also a range of architectural ironmongery and other building products on offer, though the more valuable items are only offered for sale (albeit still at a fraction of the original selling price).

If you're the kind of scavenger that likes to feel their quarry, it's also worth visiting reclamation yards for bargain materials, though these places are a bit more canny than your average construction firm and the prices are often hiked accordingly.

ADVANTAGES: A good, cheap (or even free) source of landscaping materials, and a very fair, satisfying exchange.

DISADVANTAGES: Few people have the capacity to transport the quantities of material involved.

INITIAL/ONGOING OUTLAY: none

POTENTIAL SAVING: depending on the size and scale of project and material involved, a few hundred pounds.

FREEDOM LIVING SCORE: 8 out of 10

SECTION FOUR

CLOTHES, TOYS & OTHER ITEMS

48 GET A PC FOR PENCE

You'd be surprised what you can get just by asking nicely in this world. For example, if you go looking for a cheap PC at local independent computer stores you may just come out with something for nothing.

The reason for this sudden fit of generosity is that because of recycling laws, computer shops have to pay around £20 a time to dump old PCs traded in by customers who buy new machines. So you may be saving the shop money by offering to take one off their hands. It may also be worth asking for a second machine to locate any missing/broken bits for the first one.

Most stores haven't got time to split old PCs into bits and build refurbished machines, so the perfectly reasonable old machines are going begging. Chances are it won't be a ninja PC that plays all the latest games, more like a PC that's three to six years old with a big screen. But this should be absolutely fine for word processing and surfing the net.

ADVANTAGES: It's free for goodness sakes! What more do you want?

DISADVANTAGES: You might need a bit of computer or electrical know-how to make any necessary adjustments to your new machine.

INITIAL/ONGOING OUTLAY: none

POTENTIAL SAVING: around £500 for a new PC.

FREEDOM LIVING SCORE: 8 out of 10

49 BE A SMARTER SURFER

Online shopping is both a blessing and a curse. On the downside it comes with all the inconvenience we associate with catalogue shopping, like not being able to touch the item you're buying and having to wait in for a parcel delivery. But there are great advantages and cost-savings to be had online. Here are a few tips:

COLLECT FROM THE STORE. Some electrical retailers offer a great service for online customers which allows them to reserve a product on the internet and then collect it from the store at a fairly hefty internet-only discount. Other stores may match an online quote, so even if you plan to go into a store to purchase, it's worth your while seeing the prices online first.

CLICKING COUPONS. Before buying anything online, check if there's a money-off coupon that could save you a few pounds. Go to www.google.co.uk and search for the name of the store and the word 'coupon'. You'll have to dig around but it's often possible to locate a code that you enter during the ordering process. This may give you £5 off your first order or free postage. Many major high street stores have online 'clubs' or email newsletters that offer special deals for subscribers – sign-up is free and usually pretty painless. If you're on the lookout for free food samples, cinema tickets and other printable money-off vouchers, try sites like Free Stuff Junction [www.freestuffjunction.co.uk] and www.freeukstuff.com.

GET THE MESSAGE. Message boards are a great help online if you're stuck. Mumsnet [www.mumsnet.com/Talk] is a great online community where you'll find a classified section as well as a free section. You can also ask people if they know where to get something for free or save money. Remember, Mumsnet is for dads too. Also see the money and budgeting section on UK Parents Lounge [www.ukparentslounge.com/forum/index.php] and budgeting sites like www.greasypalm.co.uk and www.moneysavingexpert.com.

ADVANTAGES: The online shopper is a savvy shopper. Websites are always offering great deals to attract first-time users and if you can spare a few minutes to register with the sites, you'll reap the benefits.

DISADVANTAGES: Online shopping is notoriously fraught with peril. Never give your credit card details to an insecure site (you can tell a secure site because it has the code 'https' at the start of the address line and a little padlock in the bottom right-hand corner of your browser). Cheap warehousing sites are also pretty adept at losing your items in the post.

INITIAL OUTLAY: none

ONGOING OUTLAY: whatever you can't resist.

POTENTIAL SAVING: If you can rein in your spending, internet prices can be around 30 per cent cheaper than high street equivalents.

FREEDOM LIVING SCORE: 6 out of 10

50 MAKE CHILDREN'S OUTDOOR TOYS FROM DISCARDED CAR AND TRACTOR TYRES

Rather like PCs (above), old and worn tyres are more trouble than they're worth for most retailers. They must pay to have them removed, which inevitably results in unsightly stockpiles created by opportunists with a plot of land to spare and no scruples. Now, I'm not suggesting that you tackle these eyesores by going into production as a tyre sculptor, but these humble rubber circles do have a range of uses in the garden and they should be appropriated if possible.

Firstly, you need to get hold of the right type of tyre – for a child's swing you want to ensure there are no sharp edges or rough bits and you will need to clean the tyre thoroughly. Find a strong tree and some good quality rope then attach the swing to the tree, remembering to bore some drainage holes in the bottom of the swing. Tractor tyres also make excellent sand pits if you can persuade a friendly neighbourhood farmer to part with one.

But tyres have uses beyond the play park – a pile of tyres makes a good planter for your potato crop, or a decent compost surround. Again, punch some holes in the tyres for ventilation and drainage.

ADVANTAGES: As a source material for children's toys and garden ornaments, tyres are free, plentiful and can even be painted bright colours.

DISADVANTAGES: Even if you can get the tyres clean, you'll never remove the rubbery smell and that will attach itself to your little ones.

INITIAL/ONGOING OUTLAY: minimal for rope and paints.

POTENTIAL SAVING: £20-£50 on swings and pots.

FREEDOM LIVING SCORE: 7 out of 10

51 TRADE AT THE DUMP

OK, so there is the potential downside that people will start calling you Stig, and that your social life will go out of the window, but in reality trading at the dump is a very good idea. Think of it as a non-virtual freecycle.

While you usually aren't permitted to pick things up that have already been dumped, there are plenty of rich pickings to be had just by approaching people who are in the process of chucking stuff away. Assuming they don't want it any more, it shouldn't make any difference to them whether you get it, and recycling is much better for the planet after all. Some council recycling facilities do actually offer the pick of the dumped items for resale, so it may be worth checking your local tip for knock-down bargains.

It's also worth your while keeping an eye out for things that have been tossed into skips around your neighbourhood – what might be obsolete for a business is fine for an individual. Again, you might be well-advised to check with the owner before hauling anything out, but they're unlikely to stop you.

ADVANTAGES: A completely free source of useful goods.

DISADVANTAGES: Everyone else thinks you're mad.

INITIAL/ONGOING OUTLAY: none

POTENTIAL SAVING: depending on the goods salvaged, anything from a few pounds to a few hundred.

FREEDOM LIVING SCORE: 9 out of 10 (slightly too grim for a perfect score)

52 GET KIDS' TOYS FROM A TOY LIBRARY OR START YOUR OWN

For anyone who's ever spent a fortune on the latest Disney action figure only to see it discarded within minutes by a fickle toddler, toy libraries are an excellent idea. Run on similar principles to book libraries (though sometimes with a nominal fee for lending), the main difference is that these are staffed almost exclusively by volunteers who are keen to promote the value of interactive play for kids and parents alike.

The main advantage is that your child gets access to a range of decent toys without the usual costs – it's a very secure sharing environment, which is also pretty useful for a child's emotional development.

To find out if there's a toy library in your area contact the National Association of Toy and Leisure Libraries (NATLL) on 020 7255 4604. And if there isn't one, ask the NATLL for details of how to start your own.

ADVANTAGES: Kids get bored with toys very quickly, so a wide library of varied toys makes perfect financial and educational sense.

DISADVANTAGES: None.

INITIAL/ONGOING OUTLAY: minimal.

POTENTIAL SAVING: £250 per year in rejected toys.

FREEDOM LIVING SCORE: 9 out of 10

53 REGISTER FOR ONLINE SURVEYS AND PRODUCT TESTING

Online market research is another boom industry, with a number of sites offering small rewards in exchange for your opinion on a variety of subjects. A couple of the most popular sites are www.toluna.com and www.valuedopinions.co.uk which both give cash rewards to survey respondents. Toluna.com also invites selected members to try out products. The rewards typically range from 75p to £1, although you have to collect a minimum level of rewards (around £10) before you're actually sent the money in the form of a voucher.

So it's not a get-rich-quick scheme, but if you have some spare time on your hands and a fast internet access it's a good way to get paid for telling someone else what you think.

ADVANTAGES: The more involved you get, the more surveys and products you are given. It's quite an interesting way to find out what companies are planning.

DISADVANTAGES: The surveys are often very repetitive and slow.

INITIAL/ONGOING OUTLAY: none.

POTENTIAL SAVING: anything from £10 to £50 per year, depending on how often you take part.

FREEDOM LIVING SCORE: 5 out of 10

54 TAN YOUR OWN ANIMAL SKINS TO MAKE LEATHER GOODS

Now we're really getting back to nature. If you've got the stomach to kill and butcher an animal and flay the hide from its carcass, then you're well on the way to being able to produce your own high quality leather goods. Even if you can't bear the idea of all that butchery, you may be able to find a slaughterman who will prepare the hide of your slaughtered goat or sheep. You can even use rabbit skin for clothes and shoes.

The three basic types of home tanning are known as brain tanning (so-called because it uses a combination of wood smoke and emulsified oils in the tanning process and one of the most common natural sources of this oil is the brain of the departed animal), bark tanning and chemical tanning.

Brain tanning is the most popular of the above methods as it produces effective results in a matter of days, though not many people are brave enough to use brains in brain tanning any more and prefer to buy their emulsified oils elsewhere. Animal hide that has been brain tanned is called buckskin, a versatile, breathable material that is also washable, and so makes great outdoor clothing.

Bark tanning takes longer and produces a stiffer resulting product, and chemical tanning produces similar results to brain tanning, though in a less 'natural' way. For more information, take a look at www.braintan.com

ADVANTAGES: Leather and hide clothes, shoes and bags are tough and durable. It's the ultimate reuse of animal waste products.

DISADVANTAGES: Buckskin is tough, but not waterproof. You need a strong stomach to prepare the hides.

INITIAL/ONGOING OUTLAY: cost of oils or chemicals, £10-£15.

POTENTIAL SAVING: £50-£100 on a good winter coat.

FREEDOM LIVING SCORE: 7 out of 10

55 MAKE FURNITURE FROM JUNK

Almost all discarded materials can be reused as furniture, home decoration or as garden ornaments. Anything that you can source from building sites, timber yards, beaches and skips that you can't or won't use as fuel can be put to good use as building material.

Driftwood, for example, is a very versatile source material. Not necessarily strong enough in itself to form the structural basis of a chair or table, it can be used creatively and cosmetically to give a finish to a piece of furniture – a driftwood-topped table for example, or driftwood cladding for a bookcase or wardrobe.

Found items like shells and broken pottery can be set together to create a mosaic effect that covers a pot table constructed from a more rudimentary material, like a broken down pallet for example. The simplest, most functional wooden or plastic chair can be rescued with a padded patchwork throw of brightly coloured fabric offcuts from a textile store.

In fact anything that can be safely cut, shaped or moulded can be put to a more practical use, from pebble doorstops to plastic sheeting table mats via coathanger topiary trainers and papier mâché picture frames.

ADVANTAGES: Reusing found materials in the home is a fun creative activity, and it's virtually free.

DISADVANTAGES: Obviously, you'll need some creative skills, and some decent tools which might offset the cost benefit of reusing junk.

INITIAL/ONGOING OUTLAY: none.

POTENTIAL SAVING: £200-£500 per year on furniture.

FREEDOM LIVING SCORE: 8 out of 10

56 MODIFY AND MAKE YOUR OWN CLOTHES FROM CAST-OFFS

If you've really got the creative bit between your teeth, you could try your hand at making your own clothes. Again, a degree of skill is required, and if you don't want to be spending long hours over the same shirt, you'll probably need to invest in a sewing machine too.

Making dresses, shirts, skirts and trousers is a bit of a dying art, but that fact weighs in your favour. Material (especially when bought from a market or textile factory shop) can be extremely cheap and you can pick up basic patterns for pence from charity shops. Try looking online for free patterns and templates as well.

If you're not quite so adept at sewing or knitting, but you still want to save money on clothes, consider modifying plain clothes from a charity shop or from a textile store. A simple embroidered pattern turns a bland T-shirt into a unique piece of clothing, even sewing accessories to a plain top, skirt or trousers can give them a serious lift.

ADVANTAGES: Another creative, frugal art form – developing the ability to sew also enables you to repair clothes and extend their usefulness.

DISADVANTAGES: Hand-sewn fabrics aren't always as hard-wearing as commercially produced items, so if you're aiming to make clothes for everyday use, you might have to get used to running repairs.

INITIAL/ONGOING OUTLAY: cost of fabrics, cotton, sewing accessories, £100.

POTENTIAL SAVING: £200-£500 per year on clothes.

FREEDOM LIVING SCORE: 7 out of 10

57 GROW YOUR OWN DYES FOR CLOTHES

If you're serious about making your own clothes from scratch it also makes sense to grow the natural products that can be used to dye the finished items. As a general rule, it's easy to guess which plants and berries make good dyes by their natural colour, but some produce more effective dyes than others. Here's a brief outline of some common natural dyes:

PLANTS AND FLOWERS: Onion skin (orange), roses and lavender (pink), red cabbage (purple), spinach, nettle (green)

BERRIES: Strawberries, cherries (light red/pink), juniper (brown), elderberries, mulberries, blackberries (all purple)

Chop the flowers, leaves or berries and boil in a pot with two parts water to one part ingredient. Strain after an hour or so of gentle simmering. Before adding the material, soak it for an hour in a fixative of salt and water or vinegar and water, rinse and then place the material and the dye together in a dye bath. Leave to soak until the required colour is achieved.

ADVANTAGES: For a truly organic experience, you can't beat home-dyed, homemade clothes.

DISADVANTAGES: Home-dyed materials must be washed separately in cool water, which makes laundry a pain.

INITIAL/ONGOING OUTLAY: minimal.

POTENTIAL SAVING: £100+ per year.

FREEDOM LIVING SCORE: 7 out of 10

58 DON'T PAY TO HAVE STAINED CLOTHES OR FURNITURE PROFESSIONALLY CLEANED

Natural, simple stain removal is a lost art, like pinhole photography and making crystal radio sets. But unlike these other pursuits, there's actually some point in learning how to get stains out of a huge range of items easily, quickly and, above all, cheaply. Esme Barber, an expert in stain removal, recommends the following tips:

To get **candle wax** off a carpet, wait until it has hardened, scrape off as much as you can and then, using a cool iron and a piece of brown paper or blotting paper, iron the paper onto the wax, which draws out the greasy residue. Freeze **chewing gum** stuck on carpet or rugs with an ice cube and then chip it off.

To get rid of **grass stains** on non-washable fabrics, use a paste of warm water and cream of tartar. To remove **blood stains** from clothing, soak the fabric in warm, salted water, and to remove a **red wine stain** from a carpet, douse with white wine. To cover a **scratch** on a table, use a paste of coffee and water. To remove a minor **carpet stain**, cut a potato in half and rub the fresh half directly onto the stain.

If you've got a **table** that's stained, greasy or oily, rub tea over it and the tannins will draw out the grease. Similarly, you can use weak tea to clean stained **mirrors**. To clean tarnished **copper** use a mixture of vinegar and salt.

ADVANTAGES: These cheap stain removal tips save a fortune on dry cleaning for clothes and professional cleaning for carpets and rugs. Most expensive chemical products are no more effective than the remedies above.

DISADVANTAGES: none.

INITIAL/ONGOING OUTLAY: minimal.

POTENTIAL SAVING: £50+ per year on cleaning products.

FREEDOM LIVING SCORE: 8 out of 10

59 MAKE YOUR OWN CLEANING PRODUCTS

About ten years ago, when daytime TV turned us all into obsessive cleaning monsters, someone remembered (probably after a freak accident in a chip shop) that vinegar was a magic ingredient.

You can use it to clean windows, floors, furniture; anything that's afflicted by a layer of grime (but don't use it on teenagers). The cleaning product manufacturers quickly got wise and tried to pretend they'd invented the craze by introducing new 'with vinegar' products left, right and centre. These were swiftly replaced by 'orange essence' or 'lemon zest', which have the distinct advantage of not smelling like vinegar.

But the essential message remains the same – the acids in vinegar (acetic) and citrus fruits (citric) are good cleaning agents, as is that other 'wonder product' baking soda. Mix these cheap and easily available items with a little water and give expensive cleaning products the heave-ho. Esme Barber offers more top cleaning tips using vinegar and baking soda:

Baking soda, mixed in equal parts with vinegar and water, produces the most effective **sink and drain cleaner** – shifting fat, food and even hair.

Rather than buying fabric deodorants, **freshen cushions and settees** that smell smoky by sprinkling with baking soda and then leave for a couple of hours. Brush them off and the smell should be gone.

If you drop something pungent like **sour milk**, douse it with vinegar which will (ultimately) neutralise the smell.

And finally, if you want a cheap and effective alternative to **toilet cleaners**, look no further than a bottle of cheap, flat cola. It really does work wonders.

ADVANTAGES: Commercial cleaning products are a chronic waste of money. These perfect substitutes cost pence and they're just as effective.

DISADVANTAGES: Vinegar has a pungent smell, especially when used as a floor and surface cleaner.

INITIAL/ONGOING OUTLAY: 30p-50p a time for vinegar or value brand citrus fruits.

POTENTIAL SAVING: up to £100+ per year on cleaning products.

FREEDOM LIVING SCORE: 8 out of 10

60 ONLY SUBSCRIBE TO FREE TRIALS FOR SUCH THINGS AS DVD CLUBS

Free or cheap DVD subscription clubs have sprung up all over the place in recent years, rather like the book and video club boom of the 1970s and 80s.

Like their forebears, these clubs work on the theory that momentum and the pace of life will stop you cancelling the contract before the end of the free trial. But some of them actually offer incentives – money or free DVDs – to take part in the trial, effectively paying you. There is no contract or obligation to stay involved.

If you're really careful with your timings, and make a note on your calendar of the exact date for cancellation, you can exploit this and try the service for nothing while pocketing the freebie. Of course, there is an outside possibility that you'll decide to keep the service anyway.

ADVANTAGES: It's a rare example of marketing actually working in your favour in an (almost) foolproof way.

DISADVANTAGES: As the club has your contact details it will bombard you with offers to retain your custom after you've cancelled. Of course, that disadvantage may work in your favour if you decide to take them up on a good deal.

INITIAL/ONGOING OUTLAY: none (though you may have to give them your debit or credit card details as part of the enrolment procedure).

POTENTIAL SAVING: they pay you – or at least give you a DVD. What a result.

FREEDOM LIVING SCORE: 8 out of 10

61 SELL YOUR HOME WITHOUT AN ESTATE AGENT

This one is a real challenge. There are two ways of looking at estate agents – they are either incredibly useful middle-men who ensure the complex transaction of a house sale goes smoothly and without confrontation, or they are a thorough pain in the neck designed to complicate a simple process for their own financial ends. Having moved house myself several times, I'd say they are actually somewhere between the two, but whatever your definition of an estate agent, you'd be hard pressed to find anyone willing to buy or sell a house without one.

The question you need to ask is why? Here are the main reasons:

ESTATE AGENTS PROVIDE A DEGREE OF SECURITY. They aren't permitted to make false descriptions of properties, but in reality this liability extends as far as a tape measure, as they have to give accurate room sizes and that's about it. Most agents specifically distance themselves from any responsibility for checking appliances and services, and they have no interest whatsoever regarding legal ownership of a property. So any potential buyer can overcome this first objection by checking the measurements for themselves.

ESTATE AGENTS HAVE A CODE OF ETHICS. Well, hopefully we can all lay claim to having ethics, even though we don't all write them down. Unfortunately, it's natural to mistrust the person you're dealing with, which is why both sides need a good solicitor (no financial shortcuts here, I'm afraid, unless you're married to one). But again, estate agencies don't really earn their crust as beacons of virtue.

ESTATE AGENTS HAVE THE BEST MARKETING REACH. This one's hard to argue with. Estate agents spend a lot of money on advertising both in print and on the web and they are a powerful force to contend with. They may seem fiercely competitive, but they are actually pack animals, preferring to band together in big online enclaves like rightmove.co.uk and primelocation.com. In the newspapers, the story is the same, with dedicated property sections that are filled with seductive ads.

So in brief, it you want to go it alone, you have two options. You can use a low-key web-based service that will charge you around £50 for a basic package of a photo and listing on a website. You pay more for a 'For Sale' board and other extras. Or you can go it alone, make your own sign, website and newspaper ad, as well as copies of details to hand out to prospective buyers. Even though you aren't subject to any regulation as a private seller, do be as honest as possible on the details – it will save hassle later.

ADVANTAGES: Estate agents' fees are huge, from 1.5 per cent right up to 3 or 4 per cent of the sales value of your house. By doing it yourself, you keep hold of the process and the communication channels.

DISADVANTAGES: It's a lot of work, especially if you aren't comfortable negotiating and getting tough on price. There's still a lot of sheep-like resistance among buyers who assume you must be working some kind of con, so it may take much longer to sell.

INITIAL OUTLAY: from £50 for a serviced package. If you do it all yourself then expect to pay around £100+ for one week's newspaper advertising plus £50 for literature and £50 for your web costs.

ONGOING OUTLAY: none, if the advertising works, otherwise it's fair to assume you'll need to spend an extra £100-£150 every six weeks or so to keep interest going.

POTENTIAL SAVING: on a £200,000 house, with 2 per cent fees, you should make a saving of around £3,500.

FREEDOM LIVING SCORE: 7 out of 10

62 GO TO TRAINING HAIR SALONS AND EAT AT TRAINING RESTAURANTS

If you've got a technical or vocational training college near you, the chances are it will have a trainee hairdressing salon and a trainee catering school. Both of these are a rich seam of young talent, eager to try out their new-found skills on willing guinea pigs, sorry, members of the public.

The salons and training restaurants are often open and available to the public during regular hours in term-time. The restaurants sometimes have special theme nights – like Valentine's and Christmas meals – or gourmet nights where the young chefs flex their culinary muscles.

The great upside of all this vocational endeavour is that much of it is carried out at a fraction of the price of normal service. The hairdressing trainees and the chefs work under the strict guidance of their instructors, so you also know you're getting an excellent level of service. Check your local college's website for details of opening hours and special events.

ADVANTAGES: You could be the inspiration for the next Nicky Clarke or Gordon Ramsay.

DISADVANTAGES: These are popular activities, so there's a lot of demand. Remember it's a training activity so you may have to be patient. In the unlikely event that you get duff service you might end up with hair that looks like linguini and linguini that looks like hair.

INITIAL/ONGOING OUTLAY: half the cost, or better, of the same services in the high street.

POTENTIAL SAVING: £10-£20 per hair appointment/£15-£30 per meal.

FREEDOM LIVING SCORE: 6 out of 10

63 GET SHAREWARE OFF THE INTERNET

There seems to be a plethora of free software available on the internet, but as a general point you should be careful before downloading it to your PC. So-called 'free' software that you can download from the web often – but not always – comes with spyware that uses up valuable resources on your PC and secretly reports back to a website about your surfing habits (so the website owners can bombard you with spam/junk emails). Free software has been known to contain viruses too.

Microsoft charge a small fortune for their Office suites. Open Office [www.openoffice.org/] from Sun Microsystems is a free alternative with many similar and compatible applications for word-processing, slide presentations and more. It's 100 per cent free – and it's a top-quality product used by major businesses.

Security companies will often provide free versions of their software for home users (not for business), saving you from shelling out £30-50 a pop to protect your PC. Try Avast! [www.avast.com] for anti-virus protection, Zone Alarm [www.zonealarm.com] for a firewall and Spybot [www.safer-networking.org/en/] for squishing spyware. You may have to look around the menus to find the product that's free to home users.

ADVANTAGES: Avoid the trap of expensive and bug-ridden 'popular' software products and still get the same user benefits. That's smart surfing.

DISADVANTAGES: Sorting the wheat from the chaff. On the internet there's so much chaff and much of it will do your computer harm, so if you're at all suspicious about a download, avoid it.

INITIAL/ONGOING OUTLAY: none, although some products may be available as time-limited trials only. You are not obliged to buy the full version after the trial has finished.

POTENTIAL SAVING: Depending on your software needs, anything from £250-£1,000.

FREEDOM LIVING SCORE: 7 out of 10

64 STAY COOL IN THE SUMMER WITHOUT AIR CONDITIONING

In the light (or should that be gloom) of recent British summers, it might seem farcical to suggest that air conditioning is a necessary component of any home, but it wasn't so long ago that we were racking up temperatures of 100F on a regular basis. The increasing popularity of sun rooms and conservatories means that the average UK house has the capacity to become incredibly hot in the summer months, and that can mean danger for anyone, old or young, who can't regulate their own heat so well.

So how do you stay cool without investing a fortune in a cumbersome and noisy air conditioner? The first thing to remember is that, as your house traps the heat, so it also traps the cold when the sun goes down. So open windows and doors between sundown and bedtime to draw in cool air, then seal it in by closing everything up tight overnight. The cool night air will keep the heat at bay for a while at least in the morning.

The second thing to remember is that if you can't cool your room down, you can at least cool yourself. Drink iced water regularly in hot weather – it keeps you hydrated and moderates your temperature. Keep a plant sprayer in the fridge filled with water and give yourself a quick misting if you get too warm; again this will keep you cooler without having to jump in a cold shower.

ADVANTAGES: Air conditioned houses, like air conditioned cars, are invariably sealed boxes which circulate bad air. They aren't healthy places – much better to keep a natural flow of air whenever possible.

DISADVANTAGES: If you open your house up at night, you'll attract all sorts of little bugs and beasties. Go the American way and fit a fly-screen to any open doors and windows – they let air in but keep pests out.

INITIAL/ONGOING OUTLAY: minimal.

POTENTIAL SAVING: air conditioning unit + power = £200-£500 minimum per year.

FREEDOM LIVING SCORE: 7 out of 10

65 HOW TO ENSURE YOU ENTER COMPETITIONS YOU ARE LIKELY TO WIN

How often have you said: "I never win anything"? And how many competitions do you enter? One, maybe two a year, I'd guess. Success in competitions, like most things in life, depends on a combination of luck, judgment and probability. Here are some valuable tips on how to maximise your chances of success:

DON'T THINK TOO LITERALLY. If a competition offers something popular, like a holiday or a trip to a spa, everyone will want a piece of it and your chance of winning is severely diminished. If the competition is for a set of coins commemorating the opening of the Telford bypass, not so many people are going to want this, and so your chances are improved. So far, so simple. But someone will want the product ultimately, so if you enter and win, you'll have something to trade. A coin collector may pay handsomely, or may swap the prize for something you do want. So never turn your nose up at the chance to win a prize, however ridiculous it may seem.

INCREASE YOUR ODDS. On a similar logic to the above, if the *Daily Mail* is giving away a speedboat, two million people will see this offer and a small percentage will try to win it. If the Bognor Times is giving away two pantomime tickets, about a thousand people will see it and only a couple will enter. In my newspaper days, competition winners were rarely chosen at random, as this increased the likelihood of the same old names getting every giveaway, such was the paucity of entrants. So enter smaller, less well-publicised competitions in local newspapers and promotional brochures. Radio competitions are often under-subscribed as well.

AIM HIGH. Though it might seem a complete contradiction to the above points, there are never as many entrants in seriously fancy competitions as you might expect. This is because people are natural pessimists and assume that the bigger the prize – like a car, or a trip to the moon – the less their likelihood of winning, so they don't bother. That can significantly increase your odds.

USE YOUR LOAF. If you have a particular gift for words and can craft a well-made rhyme or slogan, use this skill in those 'say why you like our outboard motors in no more than 250 words . . .' competitions. Always make sure the slogan you devise is a good match with the product – and don't be tempted to employ a scattergun approach here. Take your time and do each entry from scratch. A successful slogan is a carefully wrought combination of rhyme and rhythm, which must work as a spoken statement as well as a written one.

Humour is another vital ingredient of a winning slogan. Remember that your competition entry will be read by a human being, or at least by an editorial assistant. They have feelings too, and if you make them laugh then you're already half-way to that fortnight in the Bahamas.

ADVANTAGES: There are many free competitions around. Enter as many as possible, as you'll lose nothing and by the nature of probability, you'll end up with something worth something to someone. For free.

DISADVANTAGES: Once you start entering competitions it can become addictive. Many come complete with time-consuming customer surveys, so it's worth checking whether you need to do the survey to qualify for the prize. In fact you should always check the small print just to be sure you aren't committing yourself to a lifetime of spam emails or junk post.

INITIAL/ONGOING OUTLAY: none.

POTENTIAL SAVING: thousands, if you're lucky.

FREEDOM LIVING SCORE: 8 out of 10

66 HAVE A 'PRESENT AMNESTY' WITH FAMILY

A present amnesty means that you and your nearest and dearest (or at least your siblings) agree that no one will buy presents for each other, consequently saving everyone money.

This is very much a matter of personal taste; some people put a great deal of effort into the presents they buy for family on birthdays and at Christmas. Most of us just get something from the Body Shop or the off-licence at the last moment and hope it will do, which rather defeats the object of buying presents in the first place.

You have to be brave to initiate negotiations about a present amnesty, just in case your sister-in-law has come to depend on the honey and coconut bath bombs you've given her every year for a decade, but frankly most people will be relieved that there's one fewer present to buy when the festive crush comes around once more.

You could suggest a more communitarian alternative, such as a huge family party (see pot luck dinners above) instead of present-giving. That allows everyone to feel that they've made a special effort without being out of pocket.

ADVANTAGES: Avoids the unpleasantness of having to graciously receive awful presents. Also cuts down on Christmas shopping.

DISADVANTAGES: Introducing the concept could make you appear a touch Scrooge-like. Best approach is to say "Hey, everyone, I was talking to a friend and they've come up a fantastic way to be caring and save money ..."

INITIAL/ONGOING OUTLAY: none.

POTENTIAL SAVING: this depends on how generous you've been in previous years, but even at a conservative estimate it'll save you £100-£200 per year.

FREEDOM LIVING SCORE: 9 out of 10

67 LEARN HOW TO SPOT COLLECTABLES AND BARGAINS AT BOOT FAIRS

If ever there was a grim microcosm of life, it's the boot fair. They're more accurately described as table-top sales as there aren't many people who sell direct from their car boots, or sell their car boots, or sell boots. However, the phrase boot fair does sound a little like boot camp, and it would serve you well to regard it as a military exercise.

Some of the best buying at boot fairs is conducted before the tables are loaded. Swarms of bargain hunters collect around the unloading vehicles and try to pick off the best bits before they're even unboxed. If you fancy joining this pack of desperadoes, you may get an early deal from an inexperienced trader looking to cover the cost of their pitch. But an early deal isn't necessarily the best deal. No self-respecting car-bootee would sell to these vultures, but it will pay you to hang around in earshot, as you'll get an idea of what's worth fighting over later.

It's far better to take your time and be patient. Assess the various traders – some will be experienced pros but others will be occasional traders, or even boot fair virgins. This is where to focus your efforts, as they'll have little knowledge of the value of their items and/or may be willing to sell everything just to get shot of it.

In terms of the items to choose, focus on specialist items like sailing and camping equipment and sporting accessories. These big-ticket items might be evidence of a hobby gone sour and you could get a massive saving. It's always worth taking a punt on art, sculpture and ceramics, especially if the former is an original artwork, or if the latter has a maker's mark. Books and older hand tools and garden tools can also be good buys.

Finally, in the words of Eric Idle, you've got to haggle. It would be criminal not to.

ADVANTAGES: Boot fairs offer the cut and thrust of the open market, the community spirit of a recycling network and the smell of fried onions. Where else can you get all three?

DISADVANTAGES: If you're tempted to buy electrical goods or suspiciously cheap DVDs, you're about to get ripped off. Some electrical stuff may be OK, but you'll never get the chance to bring anything back.

INITIAL/ONGOING OUTLAY: it can be fun to set a small budget (say £10) and see how much you can make with it.

POTENTIAL SAVING: you can easily make ten times your outlay on the right item.

FREEDOM LIVING SCORE: 7 out of 10

SECTION FIVE

HOLIDAYS, LEARNING, WORK & LEISURE

68 GET FREE ADULT EDUCATION TRAINING

One of the greatest regrets that most people have later in life is that they didn't capitalise on learning possibilities when they were young. But it's easy to see why people might want to shy away from further education given horror stories of student debt and costly tuition fees. So it might be sensible to assume that living for free and studying on a structured course are incompatible pursuits, right? Wrong, go to the back of the class.

The basic rule of thumb regarding free adult education is that the more you need it, the cheaper it is. If you want to study the mating habits of elephants in the Thai jungle, you'll have to fork out for it yourself. But if you want to improve your literacy, maths or even foreign languages, there's plenty of free help available. Learn Direct is one of the UK's largest providers of training for adults, both privately and through the workplace. While many of the vocational courses do have a charge, free literacy and numeracy programmes are available.

Depending on where you are in the UK, other sources of free help may also be available, such as Cornwall's excellent Link into Learning scheme and similar services operating in Wales and Scotland in conjunction with the regional assemblies. In some towns and cities of the UK, regional BBC offices have Open Centres, which combine open internet access with free courses on a range of multimedia skills – visit www.bbc.co.uk/bus for more information. The BBC also offers basic online training in literacy, numeracy and languages, and there are various internet-based providers of training [such as www.creatingcareers.net] which offer free courses in a variety of vocational subjects.

If your aim is less vocational and more educational then the Open University has launched an excellent, entirely free service to all, called Open Learn. While participants don't study for a specific qualification, they are able to access a huge catalogue of the university's materials, and participate in structured units of study, forum-based discussion groups as well as keeping a learning journal that allows the individual to track their own progress through a subject. While the scheme can be seen as a recruitment drive for the university's fee-based courses, it's also a very worthwhile exercise in open access learning in its own right.

ADVANTAGES: If you're looking to change jobs and/or if you have specific literacy or numeracy needs, these free courses are a great way to change your life without spending a penny. Most of the courses can be taken online, which means they are convenient and can be built around a busy life.

DISADVANTAGES: Most free training is limited in scope and is useful only to those with fundamental learning needs. General online resources are useful and expanding, but of course they are dependent on computer literacy and internet access (to access free training in both, see libraries in section one).

INITIAL/ONGOING OUTLAY: zero for basic literacy and numeracy training, other training courses may charge fees dependent on status.

POTENTIAL SAVING: difficult to put a value on training, but you could save around £500 - £1,000 on private training costs.

FREEDOM LIVING SCORE: 8 out of 10

69 GET A GRANT OR BURSARY TO STUDY LATER IN LIFE

If you're looking for more structured or academic study, but you still want to avoid the fees, there's plenty of help and support available. In this case, the amount of support you receive will be directly related to factors such as age, previous educational experience, geographical location and income, but the sheer volume of support available to anyone who shows a commitment to return to education means that there is almost certainly some form of help for everyone in the form of a grant, loan or childcare subsidy.

A good first port of call is the Educational Grants Advisory Service [www.egas-online.org], which provides free advice and information on funding for education and training from 16+ including loans, grants, benefits, access funds, hardship funds, bursaries and charitable trusts. Also worth checking out is www.offa.org.uk – an independent public body that aims to provide fair access to higher education for all.

Individual training bodies like City & Guilds and Lifelong Learning offer money or bursaries to adults wishing to return to learning. Conditions and application criteria differ between organisations – though again the EGAS should be able to help provide full details of charities and other bodies offering help.

If you're a member of a trades union or a professional organisation, you may find another way into education through one of their bursaries or scholarships. A number of the students at Oxford's Ruskin College, a leading centre for adult education in the UK, have their studies part-funded in this way. Ruskin, which has been providing training and academic courses for a century, offers lots of information and advice for potential students who need help with fees.

In certain cases, adult learners can even qualify for a maintenance grant as well as the cost of their tuition fees – check with your local education authority for more information on discretionary grants. All in all, it pays to take a 'gap-decade' before continuing with your studies post-school.

ADVANTAGES: As an adult learner, you are more likely to be focused on your studies than the other students, who are generally just focused on each other, the dirty devils. As a way to change direction in your career or simply expand your mind, taking a serious course of study later in life can be hugely liberating.

DISADVANTAGES: If your idea of hardship is going without an olive in your Vodka Martini, then you might baulk at the thought of surviving on a grant, that's if you're one of the lucky few who qualifies for one. Otherwise you'll just have to get by on savings and your wits, which makes this an option only for the determined.

INITIAL/ONGOING OUTLAY: potentially zero, depending on status.

POTENTIAL SAVING: At least £10,000 for a degree course.

FREEDOM LIVING SCORE: 9 out of 10 (if you stick to it)

70 EXERCISE IN THE PARK AND ON THE BEACH

Going to the gym is a thorough waste of money. There, I've said it. The pointless pounds that you spend in a futile attempt to shed weight or build muscle could be vastly better spent on hiring a bike for a day, rowing on a boating lake, swimming in the sea or just running around the park with a weighted backpack. This way, you also get to avoid smelling other people's sweat and being blasted with MTV at full volume.

Seriously, parks and beaches are excellent open spaces for running, stretching and yoga – parks sometimes cater for tennis, boating and basketball at nominal cost. And now, in one Manchester park at least, they are providing serious open-air gym equipment.

Designed with older people in mind, and based on similar sites in Germany, the gym park features a range of equipment that works to tone hips, legs and upper body. A couple of hours' exercise a week should keep your average mature person lithe and fit. And the best thing? It doesn't cost a penny.

The beach is another haven of healthy reflection, especially out of season, when huge expanses of beach open up to anyone brave enough to face the elements. Kite flying, running and beach cricket are all year-round activities on the sands that will keep you ticking over better than any circuit trainer ever will.

ADVANTAGES: Parks and beaches are wonderful resources, even just for a brisk walk. Exercising in the open air makes you feel better, you get Vitamin D from the sun and fresh air in your lungs.

DISADVANTAGES: You can feel pretty self-conscious doing your press-ups in the open air. But get there early and you'll avoid the dog walkers, drunks and yobs.

INITIAL/ONGOING OUTLAY: none

POTENTIAL SAVING: if you quit the gym, you'll save at least £500 per year.

FREEDOM LIVING SCORE: 9 out of 10

71 WORK TO TRAVEL – FRUIT PICKING AND TEACHING

OK, let's define some terms pretty early on. Neither of these activities constitutes a holiday. They are good ways to get yourself to another country, and to fund your travels around that country, but in themselves, they are no picnic. The hours are long and the work is demanding.

But don't let that put you off. Take fruit, for example. Many beautiful countries of the world need seasonal labour for fruit picking – all of the great wine-producing countries for starters, but especially Australia and New Zealand. There are plenty of opportunities in Italy, Spain and Greece to help with the olive harvest, and even countries like Denmark, which you wouldn't ordinarily think of as a fruit-producing nation, are always looking out for good seasonal staff.

Teaching is more of a grey area. Most recognised schools (that is, the ones that will pay you in currency rather than magic beans) require a TEFL (Teaching English as a Foreign Language) qualification, which costs about £1,000 and a lot of hard work to acquire. Other, less scrupulous schools may take on a graduate without qualifications as long as you speak good English and look half-way presentable. You'll teach large classes, most likely of children and young adults and you'll be paid a pittance. But it's a fun way to meet people.

ADVANTAGES: Having a skill that gets you from destination to destination is a must for the dedicated traveller. The more experience you gain, the more you'll find your skills in demand – heck they might even start paying you something.

DISADVANTAGES: All the above – long hours, backbreaking work, poor conditions. You may get accommodation thrown in, you may find yourself drinking away your earnings just to get through the contract.

INITIAL/ONGOING OUTLAY: none

POTENTIAL SAVING: If you do save some earnings, these could fund a holiday at the end of your working contract, maybe up to £500 in total.

FREEDOM LIVING SCORE: 7 out of 10 (for effort)

72 GO ON A WORKING HOLIDAY

Now this is a holiday, a proper one with evenings off and nice accommodation to boot. The only downside is that you're not paid. Actually, you'll have to pay for it yourself.

The thing is, working holidays are part of the eco-industry, offering people the chance to savour a once-in-a-lifetime experience while making a contribution to the health of the planet. Far-flung holidays are available through organisations like Earth Watch, which involve participants in the ecology movement, while the fees help to keep the organisation's work going forward.

For the sake of this book's focus, we need to concentrate a little closer to home, on the budget volunteering holidays offered by organisations such as the National Trust, the BTCV (British Trust for Conservation Volunteers) and RSPB.

These holidays are for two to seven nights, and start from as little as £60 per week including food and accommodation.

But probably the biggest benefit of a working holiday is that each working party is led by a trained expert, who will pass on valuable skills and experience. Take a look at www.nationaltrust.org.uk, www.ecoholidaying.co.uk and www.wwoof.org for more information.

ADVANTAGES: Get valuable experience, meet like-minded people, get fit and pay just a few quid for the privilege.

DISADVANTAGES: Single-sex dormitories and no alcohol makes for a very different ambience to a Club 18-30 break. And it's hard work, too.

INITIAL/ONGOING OUTLAY: from as little as £60 per week all in.

POTENTIAL SAVING: over a package holiday, £250-£350 at least.

FREEDOM LIVING SCORE: 8 out of 10

73 WORK YOUR PASSAGE ON A LUXURY YACHT AS A CREW MEMBER

If you're looking to get around the world in style for free and you fancy yourself as a bit of a seadog, you can work your passage on a yacht in a couple of different ways.

First of all, there's the delivery crew. This is a pretty relaxed environment, just getting the yacht from A to B, or Antigua to Bermuda. If you're an experienced sailor you'll be well in demand for this kind of work. You may not get paid, but the trip will be an uneventful and free ride.

Then there's crewing for races, or for cruising. This can be a bit more formal, it doesn't necessarily take you in a straight line, or indeed anywhere very fast at all. It's more of a job than a travel option, and accordingly you'd expect to get paid for the privilege. You won't necessarily need sailing experience, as you may be needed for catering, waiting or cleaning duties.

Whatever takes your fancy, try a crew/yacht matching website like www.jobsonluxuryyachts.com to see what's on offer.

ADVANTAGES: Good experience and cheap travel for anyone who loves to sail.

DISADVANTAGES: There aren't that many luxury yachts flitting across the Atlantic on a regular basis. Places may be limited.

INITIAL/ONGOING OUTLAY: none

POTENTIAL SAVING: hundreds of pounds.

FREEDOM LIVING SCORE: 7 out of 10

74 GO ON HOLIDAY TO 'LIVING MUSEUMS' – AS A VOLUNTEER/EXHIBIT

There are few better things in life than getting paid for doing something you enjoy, so if you're one part thespian to two parts historian you'd thrive as an 'exhibit' in a living museum.

There's a multitude of these interactive learning experiences around the country, each of which uses seasonal staff to act as guides or to provide local colour. So if you fancy yourself as a Viking marauder or a Victorian schoolmaster, check out your options at a heritage portal like www.britainsfinest.co.uk or try the venues direct. Remember that most venues will recruit for their busy summer season in January and February.

If you just fancy getting involved on a smaller scale, museums and exhibits around the country welcome volunteers who want to give up a day or two each week to act as guides. You still get to meet people and learn new skills.

ADVANTAGES: It's a great chance to dress up, teach and have fun yourself.

DISADVANTAGES: Like all contract work, if the job starts to get monotonous, motivation can be hard. Unlike fruit picking, however, you've got to be fresh every day.

INITIAL/ONGOING OUTLAY: none

POTENTIAL SAVING: you may be given a family season ticket to the attraction you're working in, which could save a couple of hundred pounds in admission fees.

FREEDOM LIVING SCORE: 6 out of 10

75 DON'T PAY FOR A HOLIDAY – DO A HOUSE SWAP INSTEAD

House swapping is not a new phenomenon, but its popularity has only recently started to grow following a succession of daytime TV shows on the subject.

In essence, a house swap is a step up from a pen pal, in which you establish a long-distance relationship with someone until you become sufficiently secure to offer them the use of your home in exchange for theirs for an agreed period. This is a process that's made considerably easier by the advent of the internet, and well-established home-swapping companies like www.homelink.org are now big businesses, with contacts all over the world.

The length of time it takes to become confident that you'll trust someone else in your home differs from person to person. The average American may exchange homes after the first email, the average Briton may wait a few years, but generally any reservations we have about letting someone else take over our property are usually banished after the first positive exchange. In more than 50 years of operation Homelink hasn't yet had an incident of theft or vandalism.

As a rule, home exchanges only work if everyone's very upfront about what their home and neighbourhood offers when they enter their property and location details on the website. So don't be tempted to maximise the glory of life in Goole just so you'll be able to swap for a Miami condo. It's a short-term policy that will inevitably end in tears. If you can make a match with another home, always ensure that you leave your property immaculate for the new guests and that you provide copious notes with emergency contacts as well as advice on what to do and what to avoid. Take all this on board, and house swapping can become a passport to incredible foreign travel experiences.

ADVANTAGES: Home swaps are a great way to see another culture away from the usual tourist routes. If you have detailed notes of what to do and see it's as good as having the services of a local guide. And you'll never have to worry about your house being empty while you're away.

DISADVANTAGES: If you book a hotel and don't like the room, you can swap, but a house swap is fixed for the duration of your holiday, so it's important to ask any questions before you commit.

INITIAL/ONGOING OUTLAY: If you arrange the swap through a site like Homelink (which is recommended) you'll have to pay around £115 to list your property and a few pounds for a printed copy of the directory.

POTENTIAL SAVING: If you can get good flight deals, you may save at least £1,000 on a family holiday.

FREEDOM LIVING SCORE: 8 out of 10

76 BECOME A COUCH SURFER AND SEE THE WORLD (OR ITS LIVING ROOM)

A slightly odd amalgam of lift sharing and house swapping, couch-surfing is an internet craze that might involve loaning out your sofa for the night. But in return, you could get to kip in another country for free.

As the couch surfing website [www.couchsurfing.com] explains, the idea represents a new way to make friends around the world. But it's also for people who want to travel on a shoestring.

First, you look up a country on the site and find people willing to let you sleep at their property for free for one night or more. You contact them to see if this is OK and make some arrangements. They may offer you a room – or maybe just a garden where you can pitch your tent.

Having arrived, the website suggests that, in return, you help out your hosts by offering to do the washing up or other jobs around the house. Of course, the hope is that you'll also become such good friends that maybe one day you'll return the favour to your hosts. Site founder Casey Fenton says the idea has taken off at great speed, but more members are welcome – especially from the UK.

But what's to stop shady characters or anti-social free-loaders from becoming unwelcome guests in your home? Well, Fenton is aware of this risk and the site states that safety is a top priority. As a result, users can choose to become a 'verified member' so others can see they've gone the extra mile and had their name and address confirmed through credit card records and a letter sent to their home. It's also possible for couch-surfers to 'vouch' for each other, rather like providing good feedback for other members to read.

Even so, the website says it's still OK to refuse someone a couch for the night if you feel uneasy – or it's just not convenient.

ADVANTAGES: No more hotel fees or booking hassles and you may just make some good friends too.

DISADVANTAGES: You may feel honour-bound to return a favour to someone that you'd never normally dream of having in your home. And there's always an outside chance that you'll find yourself sold into slavery.

INITIAL/ONGOING OUTLAY: it's totally free to become a couch-surfer, although PayPal donations are invited.

POTENTIAL SAVING: £50-£100 per night.

FREEDOM LIVING SCORE: 8 out of 10

77 DON'T PAY FOR A HOLIDAY – BECOME A HOUSE/PET SITTER

This version of a free holiday is a bit like couch surfing with added freedom and responsibility. Your role is to make sure the house is safe, tidy and that the pets are happy for the duration of the owners' absence. This can be for a weekend, for a fortnight's holiday, or even for a much longer period of time while the owner is away. The advantages to the homeowner are clear – providing you are a trustworthy person, they have complete peace of mind. For you, it's a question of whether you're comfortable hopping from house to house and living out of a suitcase.

As with house swaps, there's a booming market in online 'brokers' for these types of service, as well as franchises that operate nationwide. Check out www.petpals.com and www.housecarers.com as a couple of popular examples. As a house-sitter advertising your services on a website, you'll have to pay a membership fee, but otherwise most of the costs involved in your stay should be covered by the person vacating the house – though don't treat this as carte blanche to start making long-distance calls.

Many people who are looking for house/pet sitters search these sites because they feel more reassured that the house sitter will be trustworthy, but there's nothing to stop you setting up alone, especially if you can do a few trial 'sits' for friends and add their testimonies to your CV. One writer that I know has been living this way successfully for the best part of a decade.

Pet sitting requires a bit more of a grown-up attitude and a genuine affinity with the animals in your care. It isn't an easy way to get a free holiday as there's a degree of chore and stress involved, though if you'd like a pet but don't want the year-round commitment, it's another bonus.

ADVANTAGES: If you can establish a good reputation you can hop from home to home and save a small fortune, especially if you move in the right circles – anyone you know who owns multiple houses should become your new best friend.

DISADVANTAGES: Unless you're very lucky, it's not necessarily a year-round occupation. House sitting can also leave you feeling rootless and insecure. Try counting the money you've saved, it'll make you feel better.

INITIAL/ONGOING OUTLAY: to register as a house sitter on a website costs around £20-£30 per year.

POTENTIAL SAVING: around £6,000-£7,000 a year in rent/mortgage and other costs.

FREEDOM LIVING SCORE: 9 out of 10

78 COLLECT AIR MILES – HOW TO GET THE MOST, QUICKEST

Owned by British Airways, Air Miles, like supermarket loyalty card points, are collected every time you spend a certain amount of money. You can earn the points on a Lloyds TSB credit card, or on a loyalty card available from the Air Miles website [www.airmiles.co.uk]. Points can be gained from other retailers and by shopping through the Air Miles online shopping section for a variety of goods and services.

Accruing Air Miles is a daunting task – the website gives an example of how to get a free flight to New York that involves spending approximately £30,000 in 12 months. If you don't rely on the Air

Miles to get you all the way to the Big Apple, you could alternatively use your Miles to get alternative rewards, such as trips out to theme parks and activity experiences.

ADVANTAGES: If you're a big spender, or a business customer, you might find yourself quickly picking up enough points for a European return flight.

DISADVANTAGES: Air Miles have suffered as a result of the general disquiet over excessive air travel. If you do manage to build up enough Miles for a flight, you'll find the range available is quite limited.

INITIAL/ONGOING OUTLAY: none for the card.

POTENTIAL SAVING: anything from £150 to £1,500 depending on your points total.

FREEDOM LIVING SCORE: 5 out of 10

79 CHECK OUT RESIDENTS' DEALS AND SEASON TICKETS AT TOURIST VENUES

Have you ever found yourself going to a particular attraction time and again? It may be because your children love the facilities, or because you love the peace and quiet. Whatever the reason, most tourist attractions around the country offer special deals for the returning visitor. Season tickets or family passes are usually double the price of a standard admission, but with frequent use they soon pay for themselves. I've used them for zoos, heritage sites and National Trust properties and they are a great way of expanding your horizons without spending too much money every time.

Another possible way to save at local attractions, whether or not you're a frequent visitor, is to check out any local residents' deals offered by the venue. Many attractions, and particularly those that rely on council or government sponsorship, have a special tariff for people who live locally. These should be clearly advertised, but as people rarely visit attractions close to home, you may have missed some incredible bargains. It's worth checking the availability of these kinds of deals with your local tourist information centre.

ADVANTAGES: If you find a place you trust and that holds everyone's attention on repeated visits, you're onto a goldmine.

DISADVANTAGES: Children are changeable souls, so choose wisely before investing in a costly season ticket. Not all activities and benefits may be open to season ticket holders – check the small print when you sign up.

INITIAL OUTLAY: twice the price of standard admission (approximately).

ONGOING OUTLAY: none

POTENTIAL SAVING: between £60 and £120 per year, depending on frequency of use.

FREEDOM LIVING SCORE: 7 out of 10

80 GET GREAT HOLIDAY DEALS BY BOOKING ONLINE

There's money to be saved on travel in a number of ways, most of which revolve around the internet (sorry to sound like a stuck record). Here's the pick of them:

BOOK LATE. Websites such as www.lastminute.com often do great deals on reduced entry to attractions as well as hotel rooms. Check the coupons idea mentioned in 'be a smarter surfer' (above) for two-for-one deals and discount coupons at tourist attractions in the UK and overseas (they are particularly popular in the US). Also visit the websites of any motorway or roadside services you may be passing. These may have a voucher page that gives you up to 20 per cent off the price of a meal.

BOOK EARLY. If you're taking an early flight or simply travelling a long distance, you can save lots of money on functional overnight accommodation by booking well in advance with Travelodge. The hotel and motel firm offers a saver rate of just £19 on rooms that are booked at least 18 days ahead of travel. You can also make incredible savings by booking train travel well in advance. Again, places and travel times may be limited. And finally, book your airport parking well in advance to save stress and money too.

ADVANTAGES: Many people focus their energies on the cost of the main holiday and forget how much the extras, like food and pre-flight accommodation, can add up. Checking these out in advance is one less thing to worry about and will save money.

DISADVANTAGES: If you book too soon, you may pay a penalty if your plans change. If you wait, there may be no availability. It's a gamble.

INITIAL/ONGOING OUTLAY: none

POTENTIAL SAVING: £50-£100+

FREEDOM LIVING SCORE: 6 out of 10

81 GET FREE TICKETS TO TV SHOWS

There are many ways to experience a live TV show: you could marry your crack-smoking mother-in-law and get on a daytime show, you could become a contestant on one of the few quiz shows that survived the 'fixing' cull. But it's far easier and more enjoyable to get tickets to the recordings of shows and it's also an extremely interesting way to get an insight into how they're put together.

For a while now, tickets to all the main shows have been available through (guess what?) a website, namely www.applausestore.com, which handles audience tickets for all of the main broadcasters – including free group bookings. The BBC still manages tickets for some of its audience radio shows [see www.bbc.co.uk/tickets].

Tickets for the most popular shows are in serious demand at both outlets. You can register on applausestore.com to get your name down for tickets, but don't be surprised if the main shows have been snapped up. The site makes its money by offering a premium 'members-only' priority booking service which costs £15 to join. This will dramatically increase your chances of getting the tickets you want. The BBC allows people wanting tickets to sign up for email updates of recording schedules.

ADVANTAGES: Watching the recording of a show can be as entertaining as a night at the theatre. There's often a warm-up act and a real sense of camaraderie as the audience works to try and build up the performances.

DISADVANTAGES: There's a lot of rubbish on TV, and you'll probably end up watching some of it live, which means it's the same rubbish, just much slower. Just as a lively audience can raise a TV show, a dull audience can kill the atmosphere.

INITIAL/ONGOING OUTLAY: none for basic membership.

POTENTIAL SAVING: on a night at the cinema and theatre, up to £30 a go.

FREEDOM LIVING SCORE: 9 out of 10

SECTION SIX

CONCLUSION

THE ULTIMATE FREEDOM LIFE – WHAT IT TAKES TO LIVE FOR FREE

Meet Ken and Barbie (not their real names). They live in London, and combine house sitting with pet sitting, and occasional couch-surfing. They haven't had a home to call their own in eight years, but then they haven't paid a penny in rent or bills either.

Ken is a carpenter and Barbie gives Indian head massages. They trade their services for goods and food. Barbie sometimes gives massages to customers in charity shops, for which the customers make a donation to the shop, and in return Barbie has the pick of donated clothing for her and Ken.

Ken was given a free laptop computer in exchange for a rather nice set of shelves he built from wood reclaimed from a demolition site and erected for his friend who runs a computer shop. Ken uses this laptop and the free internet access he gets in his house sitting residence to manage his pet-sitting and couch-surfing, to co-ordinate his LETS scheme (his management hours offset any membership fee), to trade on freecycle and to organise travel using liftshare. He and Barbie are extremely popular travelling companions via the latter, despite the fact that they can offer no financial input – Ken is an expert motor mechanic, and happily helps many of his friends maintain their vehicles in exchange for transport. And Barbie is always on hand with a head massage at refreshment breaks on long journeys. They enjoy volunteering holidays around the UK.

Ken and Barbie spend their free time exercising in the park, or reading books, newspapers and magazines in the local library. If they want to see live entertainment, they go to a recording of a TV show. They earn no money and spend no money. And yet somehow they are blissfully happy. Go figure.

OK, so Ken and Barbie are figments of my fevered imagination, but their exploits are just about plausible. When we talk about living for free, and particularly when we disparage the idea, it is always with a focus on independent living – having your own house, your own heating source, your own food source and so on.

But true freedom living isn't some survivalist hokum about living apart from society, it's about being an integral, inter-connected unit of society, but without the restraints and restrictions of financial need and want. Granted, if everyone did it there would be no houses to sit for, no yachts to crew, no cars to share. But then not everyone will do it. Doesn't stop you, though, does it?